101 BRAIN TEASERS

Harish C. Sansi

Illustrated by Strokes

Pustak Mahal®
DELHI • MUMBAI • BANGALORE • PATNA • HYDERABAD

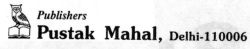

Publishers
Pustak Mahal, Delhi-110006

Sales Centres
- 6686, Khari Baoli, Delhi-110006, *Ph:* 23944314, 23911979
- 10-B, Netaji Subhash Marg, Daryaganj, New Delhi-110002
  Ph: 23268292, 23268293, 23279900 • *Fax:* 011-23280567
  E-mail: rapidexdelhi@indiatimes.com

Administrative Office
J-3/16 (Opp. Happy School), Daryaganj, New Delhi-110002
Ph: 23276539, 23272783, 23272784 • *Fax:* 011-23260518
E-mail: info@pustakmahal.com • *Website:* www.pustakmahal.com

Branch Offices
BANGALORE: 22/2, Mission Road (Shama Rao's Compound),
Bangalore-560027, *Ph:* 22234025 • *Fax:* 080-22240209
E-mail: pmblr@sancharnet.in • pustak@sancharnet.in

MUMBAI: 23-25, Zaoba Wadi (Opp. VIP Showroom), Thakurdwar,
Mumbai-400002, *Ph:* 22010941 • *Fax:* 022-22053387
E-mail: rapidex@bom5.vsnl.net.in

PATNA: Khemka House, 1st Floor (Opp. Women's Hospital), Ashok
Rajpath, Patna-800004 , *Ph:* 3094193 • *Telefax:* 0612-2302719
E-mail: rapidexptn@rediffmail.com

HYDERABAD: 5-1-707/1, Brij Bhawan, Bank Street, Koti,
Hyderabad-500095 • *Telefax:* 040-24737290
E-mail: pustakmahalhyd@yahoo.co.in

© **Pustak Mahal,** 6686, Khari Baoli, Delhi-110006

ISBN 81-223-0347-1

12th Edition : December 2004

Printed at : Param Offsetters, Okhla, New Delhi-110020

PREFACE

101 Brain Teasers is in continuation of our series of publications that have gone a longway to inculcating in our young readers a desire to acquire knowledge, keep their brain sharp and active and at the same time derive pleasure out of it. Books are no longer looked upon as something that have direct link to class-room and examination and in consequence, to be shunned when the need is over. These are now classified as friends and companions to be always carried along whether on a pleasure trip during vacations or even during a business trip. In fact, our previous publications have whipped up their appetites and they crave for more and more.

The overwhelming response to the Hindi edition of **101 Brain Teasers** convinced us of the need to present its English version also so as to reach a larger section of our young readers. While translating, care has been taken that the language used is simple and within easy grasp of the readers. A few of the riddles from the originals have been replaced by the ones which are mundane but interesting and require imagination and common sense.

This book contains a total of 101 mental exercises. Some of them are simple, some are difficult. Some are based on mathematics and some on logic. You must arrange all the facts of a riddle before proceeding with its solution.

Do not get disheartened if you are unable to solve a riddle. It will not be any reflection on your intelligence. Normally, no one can always solve a riddle. There are times when even a person with superior intelligence fumbles in answering apparently easy questions. A person's intelligence is gauged by the manner in which he can solve the problems by employing all kinds of logic, common sense and general knowledge. At times you might get stuck up. In such situations you can arrive at the correct answers by taking clue from the leads and comments provided at the end of the book.

We are sure that the book will bring forward the competitiveness in you and that you will not only feel challenged by a riddle but also derive immense pleasure in solving it. The tougher the excercise the greater will be your pleasure in finding solution to it.

Sometimes you might arrive at an ambiguous answer. In such a situation make a thorough research into it. If your conclusions are corrrect, then please write to us about it. Also, under any circumstances, do not hesitate to write to us about any doubts or queries that you may wish us to clarify. Your valuable suggestions are always welcome.

— Publishers

C haudhary Heera Chand's new farm was as strange and peculiar as were his daily dealings. He had bought this new farm at a far-off place, and for it he had to forego 50 acres of highly fertile land which he owned in the Tarai belt. This was, however, a big farm of 385 acres.

The outer walls of this new farm were worn out and were in a dilapidated condition. Heera Chand decided to rebuild the wall despite the obvious low yields. It was a strange decision considering Heera Chand's thrifty nature.

Khilavan Singh, the contractor, agreed to take on this work at the rate of Rs. 88/- per yard. He used new and good material to construct the wall and did an admirable work.

Heera Chand claimed that no other contractor could have walled the huge area at the rate he did, i.e. at Rs. 88/- per yard.

Could you tell the total expenditure incurred on the construction work? ■■

T he days of election are so hectic that the heat generated would melt the snow. Famous journalist Ravi Rai witnessed the candidates in the fray when he visited the Party office of the ruling party soon after the declaration of elections. Ticket-seekers inundated the offices of their respective parties. When Ravi Rai visited the ruling party office, he noticed a group of five prospective candidates, sitting in a corner and discussing ways and means to obtain tickets. These five—Khuda Buksh, Gurbaksh Singh, Jacob R., Param Priyadas and Banwari Prasad—were close friends. They had won their last elections from Khichadbas, Dhansai (Reserved), Peerwada, Banku (Reserved), and Sidhauda.

They had entered politics at different times and hence their experience of contesting elections was not uniform. If one was a first timer, the other was contesting for the second or third time and so on.

In the last election they had defeated their rivals by 3,54,191; 71,917; 99,998; and 1,35,971 votes. Ravi Rai collected the following information about their results:

Khuda Baksh had contested for the fourth time. His winning margin was more than Jacob but less than the winning margin of Khuda Baksh. Banwari had defeated his rival by a large margin of votes. His lone rival was Darshan

Rai whom he had defeated by 17,981 votes, making it difficult for Darshan Rai to save his security though he had managed to save it somehow.

Banwari Prasad, however, had lost to an unimportant opposition candidate in his second elections.

Banwari had never contested from Dhansai. Param Priyadas's winning margin was neither greatest nor narrowest. But he won the election securing more votes than Banwari. Param Priyadas won the election from Khichadbas.

Jacob's rival Gibson was defeated twice by Jacob earlier.

Both had never contested from Sidhauda. The candidate from Dhansai had contested only once till then.

Ravi Rai could not understand who contested from where? He was puzzled.

Can you tell :

(a)   Who defeated whom?

(b)   By how many votes?

(c)   How many times the winner had contested the last elections?

It should be remembered that the party tickets will be given to the candidates on the basis of correct answers to the above . ■■

7

Ratan had written an account of a test-match with effort. His younger brother, Shahid, a naughty chap, came and tore away some of the accounts. On the basis of rules and knowledge of cricket, please state which bowler bowled which batsman and how? Also, you have to tell how many runs that batsman scored for his team:

3. Gavaskar was caught for 46 runs from a no-ball. Surendar did not reach half-century. His wicket was taken by Mushtaq.

4. Miandad caught a batsman who had scored only 36 runs. In Chetan's score, there was no figure of 8.

5. Wicket-keeper Bari missed a

1. The batsman who was out on the bowling of Imran Khan had scored more runs than the batsman whom Harun ran out.

2. Kasim's victim was bowled. Bedi contributed only 1 run.

chance from Surendar who had scored 46 runs.

6. Kapil Dev was out for 8 runs. He was caught by Harun. Bowler Sarfraz's victim reached double figure. ■■

Double Standard

4

S eth Bagula Bhagat was a person of double standards. He would obtain thumb impression from the loanees and against a loan of Rs.10 he would invariably add a zero to make it Rs. 100 afterwards.

The loan documents were kept in a special cabinet with several pigeon-holes of different sizes and the record was maintained in a personal notebook as per the illustration below:

One day while going through his notebook, he noticed that some of the figures were blurred and were illegible.

But, the figures of loan papers kept in these pigeon-holes had inter-connection with the figures on the papers kept in other pigeon-holes also.

Can you guess how many papers were kept in all in his cabinet? ■ ■

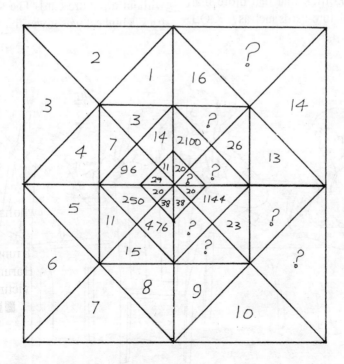

This is about the game of bridge and extremely tricky at that.

Although you have to identify from fifty-two cards you may have to tackle your brain to the maximum.

We started with 'no trump', contract call from the opponents. They made 13 tricks and the position on the table was as under:

No trick contained more than one card of the same value. There was no trick that had more than two-picture-cards such as A.K.Q.J.

The first trick's highest card was equal in value to the second lowest card in the second trick.

The second trick's lowest was higher than the second lowest in either the 4th or the 12th.

The third trick's lowest was equal in value to the highest in the second.

The fourth trick's second highest was equal to the highest in the 12th trick. The fifth trick was without a picture-card. The sixth trick's highest was lower than the

lowest in the 7th.

The seventh trick's highest equalled the second lowest in the 8th trick. The 8th, 10th and 11th tricks were identical in the value of the cards that made up each trick.

The 9th trick's second lowest equalled the second lowest in the fifth trick. The 12th trick's second highest equalled in value the highest in the 13th trick.

All four of the fives fell in successive tricks.

Six was the last card to be played. From the above would you tell what value of cards made up each of the 13 tricks?

■■

11

Last year, movies with titles *Asha, Parvana, Sansar* and *Hamare Liye* were screened in the same order as given above. The four heroes were Prem, Rakesh, Virendra, and Satish. The heroines were Yogita, Rama, Radha and Lata. The films were directed by Chopra, Tandon, Rai and Sen. The music directors were Khan Sahib, Jwala Bhai, Moni Rai and Soni-Toni.

On the basis of details given below find out the film, its hero-heroine, director and musician. (In other words, you have to find the hero-heroine, director-musician team of each film.)

1. Moni Rai gave music to the film with Satish as the hero. Rama was not in the movie.

2. As usual, Prem worked under the direction of Rai. This time Yogita was not with him.

3. Khan Sahib gave music to *Parvana*.

4. The Virendra-Radha hit movie was released before the movie directed by Sen; and after the one in which Lata had acted.

5. Musician Jwala Bhai worked with director Tandon. Chopra had discarded Lata from his films since the last two years.

6. In the film *Asha* in which Rakesh was the hero, the music for famous love duet which proved to be a super hit was scored by Soni-Toni. Yogita was not in this song. ∎

A mit Kumar was all joy when he heard that Delhi Administration was planning to have electric trains around Delhi for the 9th Asian Games. He began to dream of commuting daily in these quick moving trains from his house in Sadar Bazar to his office in Sarojini Nagar.

Previously he had travelled in electric trains in Bombay and had enjoyed the experience. Now he was looking forward to enjoying this mode of conveyance in Delhi.

For the convenience of the commuters, two types of electric-circumambulatory services were started in Delhi. Under both services the trains were starting from Hazarat Nizammuddin encircling Delhi via Tilak Bridge.

Trains of circumambulatory service No. 1 stopped at every

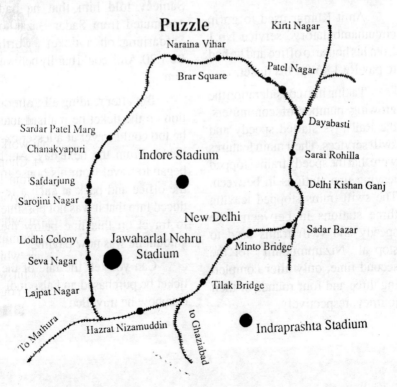

13

station. Their minimum fare was 40 paise. The average fare per stop was 13 paise.

Circumambulatory service No.2 train stopped at every alternate station. After starting from Nizammuddin station, these trains then halted at Nizammuddin after completing their 2nd round. Their minimum fare was 45 paise and fare for every stop was 14 paise only.

Amit Kumar used to go in circumambulatory service No.1 from his house to office and he had to pay Re.1.45 for his ticket.

Taking into consideration the growing number of commuters, the Railways started speedy and swift services. Their main features were that the speedy trains stopped leaving two stations in between. The swift trains stopped leaving three stations in between. The speedy and swift trains used to stop at Nizammuddin for the second time, only after completing three and four rounds of their journey, respectively.

The minimum fare of these trains was 50 paise and 55 paise respectively. The fare for every stop was 15 paise and 16 paise respectively and each ticket was of 5 paise denomination.

In spite of the introductions of speedy and swift trains, Amit Kumar commuted as before, in service No.1.

One day, when his friend Sanjeev told him that he had commuted from Sadar Bazar to Safdarjung on a ticket worth Re.1.20, Amit could hardly believe him.

But after reading all instruction on the ticket he realised that he too could travel at a lesser expense. From the next day, Amit began to travel from his house to the office and back at such a reduced fare that it was not possible to travel on this line below the amount he was now paying.

Can you tell the rate of the ticket he purchased and also indicate how he travelled? ■■

Participants from different countries had gathered for the international sports meet. Among them, the players from 'A' country were so many in number that if they were asked to form rows, the number of players in each row would be equal to the number of rows formed.

If the number of players sent by 'B' country are squared, then it would become a three-digit figure. If this three-digit figure was suffixed to the number of players sent by country 'A', then we would arrive at a six-digit figure. The square root of this figure equals the number of players sent by country 'C'.

The combined total of the players of these three countries was greater by 30 than the 1/4 (one-fourth) of the total number of participants in the games, but there was no figure 2 in the total number of participants.

Would you tell :

(a) How many players participated in the games in all?

(b) How many players participated in the competition from countries 'A', 'B' and 'C'.

■■

Lajwanti Devi of village Lajpur was a young, demure and lively woman.

Sarita Rani, her neighbour, asked her once, on seeing her with a gentleman, "What is your relation with the gentleman accompanying you?"

Lajwanti replied, "I will neither tell you his name nor my relations with him. I will, however, reveal that his mother-in-law and my mother-in-law are mother and daughter." How were these two related to each other?

■■

16

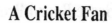
A Cricket Fan

10

On hearing about the selection of the Indian cricket team to tour Pakistan, Vinay Kumar, an ardent cricket lover, was almost mad with joy. So excited was he that he often dreamt of the matches being played, in advance. One of the dreams is as under:

1. Javed Miandad scored a century. He was caught by Gavaskar off the bowling of a fast bowler.

2. Qadir's score was in double figure. If the places of these figures are inter-changed, the new figure would be less by 45 runs than his actual score.

3. Zahir Abbas could not open his account: he was caught off an excellent delivery from Kapil Dev.

4. Imran Khan was out of Madan Lal's bowling. The runs scored by him were equal to the runs required by Mohsin Khan to complete his century, when Kirmani stumped him.

5. Javed's total score contained figure 5, while one player was run out on 8.

6. Mohinder Amarnath caught the

Captain. Madan Lal also took a catch.

7. Out of his two victims, Dilip Doshi had caught and bowled one. Mohinder Amarnath was also successful in taking one wicket.

8. The total runs scored by these 5 players included figures from 1 to 3.

On the basis of above information tell:

(a) Which player secored how many runs?

(b) Who took the wicket of each?

(c) How was each player out?

(d) Who was the captain of the Pakistani team? ■■

17

11 — The Score Board Problem

Nandkishore had burnt mid-night candles to prepare the scoreboard of the match between India and the West Indies, putting on great efforts.

In the morning, Nandkishore observed that rats had eaten away the score chart at places. He was disappointed. Can you, on the basis of given details, help Nandkishore to complete his score-chart?

The total score of Kapil's two victims, who had 'K' as a common syllable in their names was 91.

When Mohinder was returning from pavilion, he observed that the player who was magnificently caught by Shastri had scored 15 runs. Sandhu also, had taken a beautiful catch like Shastri.

Maninder's victim had scored 86 runs 5 minutes before he was caught. His name did not have 'M' in the spelling nor was he Richards, who was caught by Kirmani.

Sandhu's victim was caught behind the wickets. He could score only 20 runs.

After scoring 14 runs, Roberts hit a loose delivery. Before he could reach the bowler's end to complete his run, Gaikwad had scattered the wickets with great swiftness.

One player had scored 76 runs. Immediately on arrival, Michael holding had run two byes on the 5th ball of an over by Kapil and on the last ball of that over he took one more leg-bye. In the next over he was caught off the first delivery from Mohindra.

Lloyed was stumped. Jeff Dujon scored more runs than Marshal and was caught by Vengsarkar.

Scoreboard

1. Gorden Greenidge b Shastri 35
2. Larry Games lbw V. Raghavan 42
3. Desmond Haynes c Gavaskar b Shastri 5
4. Vivian Richards ....
5. Gus Logie c Gavaskar b Shastri 4
6. 2
7. Jeff Dujon ....
8. Joel Garner not out 30
9. Malcom Marshall ....
10. Andy Roberts ....
11. ....

Extras 27
West Indies Ist Innings, total score 357
Fall of wickets :   1-47, 2-80, 3-88, 4-96, 5-127, 6-223,
7-295, 8-316 and 9-340.

Bowling analysis

	0	M	R	W
Kapil Dev	14	3	63	2
Maninder	11.1	2	42	1
Sandhu	10	3	37	1
Shastri	16	5	93	3
Mohinder	11	4	51	1
V. Raghvan	8	2	44	1

All the Indians were disappointed when P.T. Usha could not get any medal at the Ento Olympics despite her great efforts. Similarly, women competitors Kimrochniva, Che-wang, Fu-Chin, Bezobanchanev and Masakìri disappointed the Americans, Koreans, Chinese, Romanians and Japanese when they could not get any medal at the Ento Olympics.

In spite of great efforts by these participants, they could hardly secure fourth, fifth, sixth, seventh and eighth places due to some reasons.

Bezoba's place was better than Wang's but was next to the place secured by the runner from China. The unfortunate sportswoman from America could only secure the eighth place.

The Chinese sportswoman did not participate in gymnastic. She did not get fourth place even. Wang did not take part in athletics.

Masakari of Japan participated in swimming. Korea's sportswoman came seventh in diving. One participant took part in running.

Romanian sportswoman participated in javellin and Kimrochinva took part in gymnastic.

From the above tell:

1. Which sportswoman participated in which event?

2. What was the place of each participant in an event? ▪▪

Seth Jagdish Lal has two sons. Elder son was Satyender Kumar and younger was Baljeet Kumar. Satyender was two years older than Baljeet.

A year ago, the difference in the square of their total was 84 (which was 8 years more than the age of their grandfather). Sethji purchased a new car for both of them the same year. A special kind of number plate was got prepared. The colour of the plate was black and golden electric bulbs were fitted on it shaping its letters and figures.

When this plate was ready

Baljeet mistakenly hung it upside down and observed that the numbers on it read the same as would read when held the other side up, also.

Incidentally, if the total of multiplication of Satyender's and Baljeet's age, occurring at that time, was included in the figures of the number plate, then the total would be equal to the square of Seth Jagdish Lal's present age.

Could you tell the present ages of Satyender, Baljeet and their father? Also tell what was the car number?

■■

S wadhinchand was a big industrialist. After earning a lot of money in foreign countries, he thought of starting some business in India and for that purpose, he opened an office, in Delhi.

He wanted to manufacture modern bicycles. Thinking that starting a new factory would take much time, he decided to purchase any of the existing factories, e.g. Jaire Cycle Works Limited, Tejari Cycles and Allied Industries Ltd., or Priya Cycles Ltd.

For this purpose he sent two of his officers to survey the market. Both of them submitted their reports after 4 days, as under:

Report No.1, Surveyor — Chint Raman :

He surveyed 414 houses. There were 515 bicycles. 28 houses had no bicycles at all. In 46, 55 and 62 houses there were bicycles manufactured by Jaire, Tejari, and Priya industries respectively. In 51 houses the bicycles were from Jaire and Tejari, in 19 houses from Tejari and Priya, and in 36 houses from Priya and Jaire. In 7 houses there were bicycles from all 3 companies.

Findings: The popularity of Jaire bicycles was undoubtful in market.

Report No. 2, Surveyor — Lakhan Chand:

176 houses were surveyed. They had 200 bicycles. 35 houses did not use cycles.

1/4th minus 3 houses had Priya bicycles. 25 had Jaire and 26

had Tejari. 10 houses had all the three models. 15 houses had both, Tejari and Priya and 6 houses had Jaire also, while remaining 18 houses had both, Jaire and Priya.

Findings : Priya was most in demand in the market.

After studying both the reports, Swadhinchand decided to purchase the shares of Priya Cycles Ltd., and issued orders to go ahead with that.

Simultaneously, he dismissed Chint Raman, the surveyor who was under the impression that having surveyed more houses than his counterpart he would be rewarded.

Lakhan Chand was appointed as Chief Manager (Sales).

Can you guess why Chint Raman was dismissed? ■■

23

The Railway line from Shyam Ganj to Preet Nagar ran via Parvat City.

Pravat City's old railway station was destroyed in the bombardment during World War II and its contact with Preet Nagar was broken. The new station was being utilised to keep repairable wagons and also as siding place. Since the new station was being linked with Preet Nagar, there was, however, no arrangement for the engine to turn around and return. Therefore, the train did not go up to Parvat City. It used to return from Jivan Nagar itself.

One day the station master of Parvat city observed that wagon number 'B' stationed at his platform was empty, whereas wagon 'A' at the old station was full. It was almost impossible to transport the goods from this wagon to the new railway station. An engine 'C' from Jiwan Nagar was, therefore, sent to Parvat city to bring back wagon 'A' to the new railway station and to take wagon 'B' to old railway platform. This was to be done in such a manner that the engine should have to shunt the minimum. After this shunting the engine had to return to Jiwan Nagar.

When the driver was ready to start this operation, the station master gave him a railway track

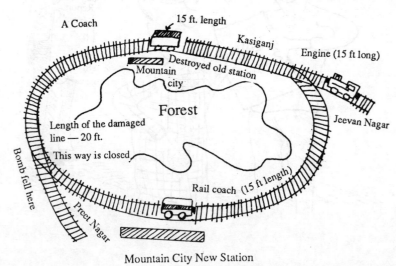

A Coach
15 ft. length
Kasiganj
Engine (15 ft long)
Destroyed old station
Mountain city
Forest
Length of the damaged line — 20 ft.
Jeevan Nagar
This way is closed
Bomb fell here
Preet Nagar
Rail coach (15 ft length)
Mountain City New Station

map (as shown in the following figure) and told him that the line going to Preet Nagar was damaged at the points 'D' and 'E' due to bombardment. The engine, therefore, would not pass through these points. Perhaps, the wagon being lighter than the engine might pass through these points.

Having seen the map carefully and observed the conditions, the driver said that under those circumstances it was not possible for him to change the places of the wagons. But, there was an intelligent man who whispered some words in the driver's ears about the ways and means to change the places of wagons. The driver smiled. He changed the places of wagons as required. How did he do it? ■■

That was an year for tourism. Mandi in Himachal Pradesh is famous for its distant temples—temples in deep forests, on top of high cliffs and where not?

So, I took a local guide and started for one. The day was hot and road, rocky at places and dusty at most.

"How far have we come?" I enquired of the sweating guide.

"Half of the distance we have yet to go," was his reply.

After another half a mile, I asked, "How far yet to go?"

"Half the distance we have already covered." Replied the guide. It made no sense to me.

I sat down under a tree and began to work out: 'How much distance would it be from starting point at Mandi to the temple'? I could not make out. Could you help me? ■■

S atish was adept at solving arithmetical problems. He had some fanciful ideas on the jugglery of figures. One day he prepared a series of problems with a view to putting his friend Shyam to test. It was quite late before he could complete the problems. So he kept the papers on the table and went to bed. A cat crept in the room at midnight and toppled the ink-pot, disfiguring some of the figures, The blurred figures could not be read as they were smudged.

Could you help Satish in deciphering the figures in columns 'a', 'b' and 'c' (see figure).

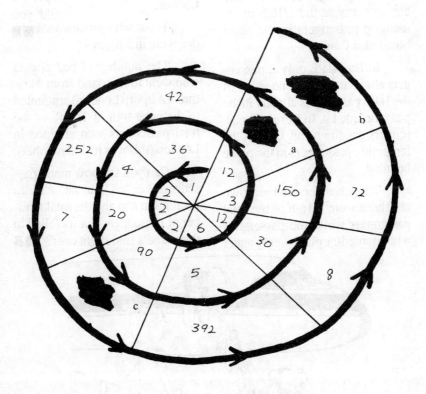

The Air India 's Jambo Jet 'Samrat' took its first ever flight from Delhi. The Delhi-London scheduled flight had seven halting stations, i.e. Bombay, Cairo, Baghdad. Beruit, Ethens, Rome and Paris.

No passenger alighted at Bombay, while 45 passengers had boarded the plane before its start. 22 passengers got down at Cairo and as many as the 1/10th of remaining passengers in the plane boarded at Cairo.

In Baghdad, only 2 passengers alighted, while one short of the 1/4th passengers already in the plane boarded it. In Beriut 89 passengers got down and 1/7th of the remaining passengers in the plane boarded.

The passengers who got down at Ethens were 1/16th of the total passengers while the passengers who boarded the plane were greater by 20 in number than the square root of the remaining passengers.

At Rome 1/4th of the passengers alighted. When the plane took its flight, then there were 10 passengers more than the total number of passengers it had earlier.

In Paris 1/9th of the total passengers alighted and only 30 passengers boarded the plane for London.

Those who got down at London were in 3 figures.

The number of passengers who went to Scotland from Heathrow Airport (London) amounted to the cube root of 1/10th of the total passengers who alighted in London (this was in odd number).

Can you say how many passengers boarded 'Samrat' at Delhi for foreign trip and the total number of passengers that travelled in this plane's first flight ever? ■■

Salam

The Fifth Column

It has been rightly said that rumours are the worst enemy of a country. They spread swiftly like a fire. This was amply evident during the war between Prem Puri and Irsha Puri.

When the king of Irsha Puri, Jalim Singh attacked Prem Puri, the soldiers of Prem Puri not only retaliated strongly but they were able to drive away the enemy also.

In order to take the revenge Jalim Singh used the famous weapon 'rumours'. He assigned two of his expert men to spread rumours. They studied the situation at Prem Puri and spread a rumour that somebody had poisoned the drinking water tank of the city. In order to spread this rumour they took into confidence two of the credulous residents of Prem Puri and told them about the poison. The spies bolted away thereafter. These two credulous youngmen started spreading this rumour and discountinued the use of the tank's water themselves. They had started their mission at 6 o'clock in the morning.

Later on, it was known that every man who received this rumour aprised two persons of it every 15 minutes and by 8.45 in the same morning there were only 1233 persons who were in dark about this rumour. Rest of the population of Prem Puri had heard about it.

Can you guess the total population of Prem Puri?

■■

Maharaj Veer Bahadur Sen was going to London on board the steamer 'Shaurya Chakra', along with his wife, Sounderyavati Devi and faithful servant Sevak Ram.

Because of the abolition of states and discontinuation of Privy Purses, the Maharaja seemed somewhat hard-up. Considering his deteriorated economic condition, he decided to sell ancestral jewels and diamonds to make up the shortage of funds. Hearing about the sale of the precious jewels and diamonds many jewellers approached him. But none of them could assess their actual value. As a result of this the Maharaja decided to go to London.

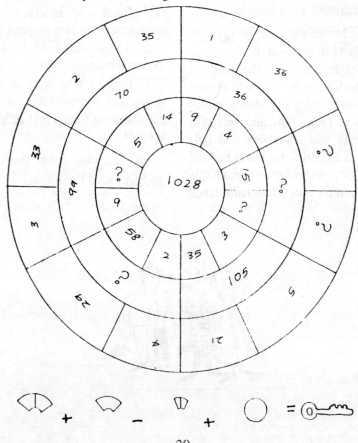

He put the valuables in a small box having numerical lock system and locked that box in a strong trunk having a key-device lock.

Due to heavy storm during the voyage the Shaurya Chakra sank and all the passengers aboard drowned into the sea. After some time, explorations to fish out the valuables of Maharaja started. The trunk containing the valuables was taken out by the divers.

Breaking of the small box, which had the numerical lock sys-tem, would have caused damage to the jewels and diamonds. It was, therefore, imperative to decipher the combination of the four-digit secret numbers of the lock.

The leader of the exploratory team suddenly found an ordinary piece of paper (see figure) out of the stuff kept in the strong trunk, which had a key-device lock. He felt happy and immediately dis-covered the combination.

Would you try to find out the four-digit secret numbers that opened the lock? ■■

Come on riders, let us know what you say?

When Diler Singh the ruler of Karmath Puri attacked Aram Pur, its ruler Manoranjan Prasad was busy in amorous affairs in his Luxury Palace situated on the hills of Aram Pur.

In order to apprise the ruler of the attack by Diler Singh, prince Shakti Singh sent his reliable soldier Ramendra Pratap to the Luxury Palace. The latter started exactly at 7 a.m. on his horse.

Precisely after 2 hours the prince assigned another soldier, Virbhadra to proceed to the palace in question. Both the soldiers reached the palace exactly at 2 o'clock in the noon. On reaching the palace they learnt that the ruler had not got up from his sleep till then.

Both the riders had taken some rest on their way to the palace. Ramendra Pratap had rested for 1/7th of the time taken by Virbhadra during his riding, whereas resting time of Virbhadra was 7 times less than the riding time taken by Ramendra Prasad. In other words the riding time of Ramendra Prasad was 7 times more than the resting time of Virbhadra.

During this journey Virbhadra rode at an average speed of 35 m.p.h. whereas Ramendra's speed was 25 m.p.h. One of the two riders had taken a shorter route?

Can you tell who went by the shorter route? Also tell the distance between Aram Pur and Luxury Palace by the longer route?

■■

The representatives of state youth club Delhi, had a meeting opposite Rajghat. To participate in this meeting other clubs, namely Dhairyashali Youth Club, Imagination Club, Vikassheel Youth Club, Aap Aur Hum and Kalpanasheel Youth Club had also come. Their representatives had come from Karol Bagh, Tilak

Nagar, Rama Krishna Puram, Rohtas Nagar and Sarojini Nagar. Their names were Imran Khan, Kailash Thakur, Jacob Smith, Ramesh Nagarath and Satwant Singh. They were accompanied by

Asha Ghosh, Geeta Singh, Mrinalini, Rama Arora and Sulabha Karkare.

Asha did not accompany Ramesh Nagarath of Dhairyashali Club. She was a representative of a Karol Bagh club.

Aap aur Hum Club was not in Ramakrishna Puram. Its representative Satwant Singh participated in the meeting. Kalpanasheel Youth Club belonged to the Sarojini Nagar's youths.

Jacob was the representative of the Vikassheel Youth Club while Geeta was from some club of Tilak Nagar. Imran and Rama belonged to the same club.

One important feature was that the first letters occurring in the names of male and female youths coming from the same place had no similarity with the first letters occurring in the names of clubs and places.

From the above can you tell which male and female youth represented which club and to which place the club belonged? ∎∎

L ast year's mathematical se- ries prepared by Satish was easily solved by his friend Shyam. This made Satish a little non-plus.

This time during the Xmas holidays Satish tried to make an- other series which was quite a brain-teaser. He left some of the columns blank. This time Shyam found difficulty in filling the blank places. Can you make it easy for Shyam and help him solve this problem?

Then go ahead, Shyam is waiting for you.

Here is your problem (see figure below): ■■

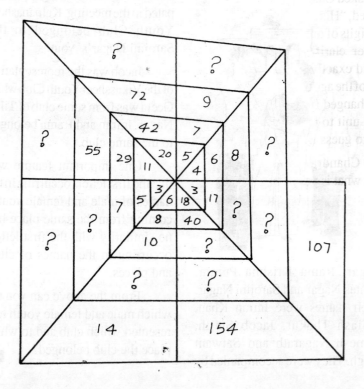

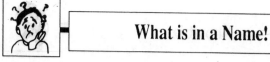

While Chandrawati was busy chatting in the house of her neighbour Saraswati, with latter's mother Sharbati Devi, Savita, daughter of Saraswati, entered with her son.

Chandrawati asked Savita the name of her son. Savita replied, "Aunty, he is Ranjan." How old is he? asked Chandrawati. Saraswati replied, "His age represents one of the digits of our Savita's age". She further clarified, "Savita's age would exactly be same if the figures of the age of my grand-mother are changed from tens to unit and from unit to tens. Now, it is upto you to guess it?".

Chandrawati again asked, "But what is your grand-mother's age?" Saraswati replied, "The total of my grand-mother's age and Savita's age is equal to the total of my mother's age and mine. Also, the figures of our ages are the same. Last year our individual ages could evenly be divided by 2. But this year our ages cannot be divided by 5. Is that clear?" "Oh, Saraswati, I wanted to know Ranjan's age and you have put a riddle before me"! quipped Chandrawati.

"Well, that is your headache. I have told you what I should have."

Now, friends, would not you like to help Chandrawati? So, just tell the age of each of them. If it is not possible for you, just tell the total of their ages. ■■

Cinema

Kenar Ke Phool

Let us have some showbiz.

The owner of Manbhavan Picture Hall, Ratan Chand had set up a trust in the memory of Guru Rameshwar Das, who was his revered mentor. He named it Guru Rameshwar Das Memorial Trust. For this purpose he gave in charity Rs. 50,000. He also declared that he would give to the trust, 5 paise per spectator for each show held in Manbhavan Hall. This way a maximum of Rs. 201 could be collected in a day.

The picture hall had four types of seats for the spectators, namely lower stall, middle stall, upper stall and balcony. The maximum shows held per day in this hall were four.

A few days back the Ambassador Music Club had organised a premier show of a multi-star film *'Sitaron-ke Aage'*. The denomination of the tickets for the show was – lower stall: Rs.10, middle stall: Rs. 25, upper stall: Rs. 50 and balcony Rs. 100.

Despite the high cost of the tickets there was unprecedented rush for the tickets and all tickets were sold three days prior to the ceremony. The club earned Rs. 51,800.

Contrary to this, during the first show of *'Kanher Ke Phool'*, the middle stall had 6 empty seats more than the lower stall. The number of occupied seats of the upper stall was 9 more than 1/4th of its total seats. The number of

Salam

tickets purchased for the balcony was 12 more than 1/3rd of its total number of seats.

The empty seats of the lower stall had the same figures in three digits and this figure was less than the empty seats of all other stalls.

The income from *Kanher ke Phool* was only 1/35th of the total income that accrued from the premier show of *Sitaron Ke Aage*. The denomination of tickets for *Kanher ke Phool* was Rs. 2.25,

Rs. 3, Rs. 4.50, and Rs. 5.75 respectively. From the above, can you guess:

(a) How many seats were there in all in Manbhavan picture hall?

(b) How many seats were there stallwise?

Lead: The total capacity of balcony's seats was equal to 3/4th minus 15 of the total of lower and middle stall's seats.

■■

B e careful. We are dealing with some family intrigues.

Havildar Ram Vilas Prasad Singh's wife delivered twins — the first born was a girl and the second was a son. They already had eight children.

Now, they had a problem naming these children. They asked all the eight of their children to fall in one line. When the children presented themselves in one line their names were asked and jotted down in order of seniority. The names were as under:

Kamala Devi, Kamta Prasad, Bela Devi, Beni Prasad, Gita Devi, Girish Kumar, Gopal Prasad, Gomti Devi.

Havildar Sahib glanced at the list of his children and found one peculiarity in it. Taking into consideration this peculiarity he named his two new-born. Their names will be found in the names given below:

Gita Devi, Gopal Prasad, Gauri Devi, Mathura Prasad Singh, Mukund Lal, Mohini Devi, Mauli Chandra Singh, Bal Bahadra Singh, Ratan Kumari, Ravindra Pratap, Raj Kumar, Raj Rani Devi, Roop Kishore, Roop Narayan, Vimla, Virbala, Shanti Devi, Sarjo Prasad Singh, Seema Kumari, Hemlata, Hotilal and Homwati Devi, Durga Devi, Dudh Nath Singh.

Can you tell what were the names selected by him for his two new-born? ■■

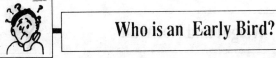

Who is an Early Bird?

27

Ramesh has an ancestral wrist-watch bequeathed to him by his grand-father. Suresh has a new watch, a gift from his girl-friend. Ramesh's watch is ten minutes slow but he thinks it is five min-utes fast. Suresh's watch is five minutes fast but he thinks it is ten minutes slow.

One day, they plan to catch a train leaving at 4 o'clock. Who would get into the train first? ■ ■

Anshul filled a large-sized tank with water and floated a big bowl in it. After that he began to drop zinc balls in the bowl one at a time. With each ball the bowl began to sink slowly. After 30 balls 3/4th of the bowl was immersed in water.

At this stage he marked the water level of the tank by putting a mark there. Meanwhile Vikas, his naughty little brother came and pressed the bowl with his hand, as a result of which the bowl sank completely into the water with the 30 zinc balls in it.

Now tell :

Was there any change in the water level which Anshul had marked? If so, how? If no, Why? You have to explain the above with reason.

■■

Ramu was moving leisurely, watching the different stalls at a fair. It was a pleasure to see the colourful display of clothes, bangles, plastic goods, ribbons and toys. But, suddenly a game stall full of cheer caught his attention. He dashed towards it. There was uncle John, his stand bearing the numbers 9, 12, 21, 26, 30, 39, 41 and 45 was to be knocked down. But, there was a special prize for anyone who could knock over figures totalling exactly 100. Which numbers Ramu should have selected in an instant? Can you tell? ■■

Shravan and Balbir were studying in the same class. Premji, their drawing teacher, gave them a design to make. Shravan was the first to complete the requisite design. His teacher congratulated him.

Sometime later, he got a brainwave and wrote down some figures in the blank spaces of the design. In some of the columns he also wrote down 'A', 'B', 'C', etc. (see figure below).

During the interval he showed that design to Balbir and asked him to put figures in place of letters in the design.

Balbir studied the design and came to the conclusion that Shravan had something special in his mind before putting the figures.

Can you guess what figures were to be written in place of 'A', 'B', 'C', 'D' and 'E'?

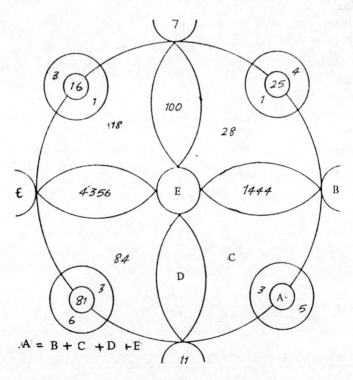

$A = B + C + D + E$

Sadashiv had a phenomenal memory.

Sadashiv had seen the car used by the killers to escape, after they had murdered Ram Charan on Sunday night. Soon after the incident the whole locality gathered and raised a hue and cry. The police arrived immediately on the spot.

Inspector Jogendar made a survey of the place where Ram Charan was murdered. He enquired from the crowd, "Has anybody seen the criminals while they were escaping?"

Sadashiv came forward and replied, "Yes, I have seen them fleeing in a red-colour fiat."

"What was the number of the car?" Asked Inspector Jogendar anxiously.

"Sir, preceded by letters DIB, the number was in four digits. All the four numbers were different from each other. The first figure was one-and-a-half times the last figure. The total of first two figures was half of the total of figure numbers 3 and 4. Also, the difference between the two middle figures was only one."

Inspector Jogendar Singh taking Sadashiv for a lunatic was about to ask him to leave the place when sub-inspector Ravinder came forward and whispered the car number into Inspector Jogendar's ear.

Taking clue from Sadashiv, the car was found and the criminals were arrested.

Can you guess what was the number of the car that Sadashiv had seen?

■■

Gagan Chumbi, the famous multi-storey building of the city accidentally caught fire. Fire Brigades reached the spot from all over the city. The most modern fire engine, Sheetal Yan, positioned itself immediately.

Ashish Parnami, the Chief Officer of Sheetal Yan selected a proper place for operation and switched on a button to raise a safety ladder. The ladder advanced like a huge serpent towards the roof of the building and within a moment it went so high that it touched a corner of the 3-storey Sabha Bhavan (see figure), adjacent to Gagan Chumbi. With the help of fire-fighters and the public of the locality, the fire was soon put out.

Now there began a discussion among all regarding the grandeur of the Gagan Chumbi. People began to speculate about its height. Lala Subhash Vig claimed that if he could be made aware of the length of the ladder and size of the Sabha Bhavan building, he could assess the exact height of Gagan Chumbi.

Yashpal who was standing near by enquired about the length of the ladder from Ashish Parnami which the latter confirmed to be 125 ft 6 inches.

The care-taker of Gagan Chumbi informed about the size of Sabha Bhavan as : 36 ft broad, 300 ft long and 36 ft high. Within no time Lala Subhash Vig told the exact height of the building in question. Not only that, he also told the distance that lay between the wall, on which the ladder had been rested, and the lower end of the ladder.

Can you tell what was, as per Subhash Vig's calculation, the height of the building and the distance in question? ■■

I llustrated below is the lay out of Lala Badri Prasad's rose garden. He asked his son Shankar to pluck some flowers to be offered to God on the following conditions:

1. The plant from which a flower is to be plucked should be third in the straight row.

2. Starting from any plant the flower should be plucked from the third plant only.

3. The plant from which a flower is plucked should not be taken into consideration to begin counting.

4. The number of flowers to be plucked from the last plant should be double the number of the flowers plucked from the earlier plant. In other words starting should be with one flower at the first plucking, the next plucking should be with two flowers, the third to be with four, the fourth to be with eight, and the fifth plucking should amount to sixteen flowers.

Can you guide Shankar in collecting the maximum number of flowers? ■■

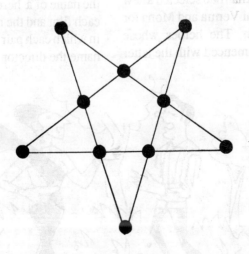

Friday was a field day for cine-lovers as five new films were released.

Films *Arpana, Chalta Purza* and *Swapana Sansar* were the three professional films. The remaining two films *Karma Dweep* and *Seva Ashram* were art films.

The heroes were Mani Verma, Mrinal Rai, Raman Nidhe, Rakesh Ranjan and Sidhanth Sharma. The heroines were Mona, Rama, Lata, Loveleen and Sapna.

The directors were Arif Khan, Pramod Goswami, Prem Tilak, Ratan Jeet and Subash Barman.

Arif Khan had selected a new pair of Mani Verma and Mona for his art film. The heroes whose names commenced with the letter 'R' were paired with the heroines whose names started with letter 'L' and they had acted in professional films only.

Sidhanth Sharma's role in *Swapna Sansar* was being appreciated everywhere. But Sapna was not his heroine.

Tilak directed the film in which Rakesh had acted. But he had not worked for *Chalta Purza*.

Mrinal Rai had not worked with Ratanjeet. His film had started after *Seva Ashram*.

Lata and Pramod's film was quite a success.

From the above can you tell the name of a hero and heroine of each film and the name of the film in which each pair had acted. Also name the director of each film.

India ended fifth in the World Cup Hockey, disappointing thousands of hockey fans. Brahma Kumar Pal was also one of them. While thinking over the pros and cons of India's defeat he fell asleep.

In his dream Pal saw the World Cup Hockey competition. After some matches the position of participating countries in league matches was:

India-10 points, Kenya-2 points, Malaysia-3 points, Russia-3 points, Spain-10 points, Australia-6 points and Holland-8 points.

At this stage Pal woke up. But he had forgotten most part of his dream. However, besides this list of points, he remembered that the matches which Holland drew were twice the number of matches it won.

Australia managed to see that none of the matches it played was drawn. The most spectacular match of this series was between Russia and Kenya in which Kenya defeated its much stronger opponent by 3 goals to 2.

With the help of your knowledge of the game of hockey and from the above details, would you tell the results of the matches played by these countries.

■■

India = 10	Australia = 6
Kenya = 2	Holland = 8
Malaysia = 3	
Rusia = 3	
Spain = 3	

`~oos 7th time only once (7 includes f

Four friends, namely Jagat Narayan, Banarasi Das, Moti Lal and Sita Ram were staying in block 'A'. Last year in January, they decided to save money during the whole year and travel with that money throughout the country. Their wives also started saving money. The total savings of the four couples in the year amounted to Rs. 25,000. The four women on their part had saved together three times of the 1/8th of the total saving.

Rukmani had saved 40% more than Lakshmi, Sushila had saved 2/3 more than what Rukmani had saved. Devi on her part had saved Rs. 175 more than Rukmani.

Among the male friends Sita Ram, Jagat Narayan and Moti Lal had saved 3 times, 2 times and one-and-a-quarter times more than their wives, respectively.

Banarasi Das could not save much. He could save only Rs.25 more than the 1/4th of the saving of his wife.

Would you please tell how mush each couple could save in all. Give their names.

Also state which couple saved the maximum. ■■

O n 10 December 1981, Inspector Bhishma Verma received an information through Interpol that some members of an international gang, which was involved in anti-national activities had checked in Hotel Yatra Vihar. Their ringleader was also there. Inspector Verma had gathered information that two days back the members of this gang had gone out of Delhi to meet their cronies at different places to collect some information that would have endangered our country's safety.

It was then that the 'operation 02' started. Bhishma Verma assigned two of his colleagues, Sunil Nagar and Balbir Yadav to collect further information about this gang with a view to arresting the criminals on the basis of their involvement.

Balbir was able to detect that the movements of Abhishek, Ashok, Nishikant, Prakash and Bhanu Pratap were suspicious. Just two days back all these five had gone to different places in the cars, owned by the hotel. The main reason for suspicion was that despite severe cold they had gone to hill stations and that too at night.

The numbers of the cars owned by the hotel were: DLZ 1001, 1980, 2134, 2222, 2618, 2692 and 3443. Their drivers's names were: Govind, Durga Prasad, Maha Singh, Meva Lal, Prem Singh, Banarasi Das and Sohan Lal.

Incidentally, plate numbers of all the cars used by these gangsters could be divided by 11.

Car No. 1980 had gone to Srinagar while Maha Singh had taken car No. 2134 to Kulu.

According to Sunil Nagar, the man who travelled in a car whose number was divisible by 7 was suspected to be the ringleader.

Some bullet marks were found on the car which went to Shimla. It seemed that it was fired at on its way.

Though Prakash had gone to

Dehra Dun, he did not use car No. 2222; nor driver Mewalal had accompanied him. Car No. 2618 was in the workshop form the last three days for repairing. Jamuna Prasad, foreman of the workshop had confirmed that driver Prem Singh was busy with mechanic Radhey Shyam for the last three days.

The criminal that travelled in Sohan Lal's car had letter 'P' in the spelling of his name. Nishikant had gone to Nainital in car No. 3443 but its driver was not Govind. Abhishek went in Durga Prasad's car but his car did not have the bullet marks. The bullet marks were also not seen on Sohan Lal's car.

The driver who drove Ashok's car did not have the letter 'M' in his name.

Banarasi Das was admitted to hospital on 7 December . Afterwards his heart was operated upon. Verma arrested the ringleader with the help of some information. Later on, with the help of other information the other criminals of the gang were also arrested.

From the above, will you state?

1. Who was the ringleader?

2. Which criminal travelled in whose car? (Give name of the driver).

3. What was the number of car in which each criminal travelled and from where was the information gathered?

■ ■

50

The Age -Old Problem — 38

O nce, Master Vasant Raj was going to Haldwani in a bus to attend the marriage of his friend Dinanath's son. His son Mahabir Prasad and naughty little grandson Arvind, were also accompanying him. Their co-traveller, Dwarka Das, during their cursory talks, asked Masterji, "What subject do you teach? Masterji replied, "I teach Mathematics."

Dwarka Das queried further, "For how many years have you been teaching in the school?"

Masterji interjected, "Years!" and began to think. Then he replied, "I have been teaching for 2/3 of my age less 3 years. And, my age today is twelve years less than half of the square of Arvind's age."

He continued, "This is my son Mahabir. The total of my age and Arvind's age is one and a quarter more than Mahavir's age."

Then he added, "When we celebrated Arvind's second birthday, my age was double the age of Arvind's age plus Mahavir's age plus 5 years. Have you got it?"

"Now can you calculate the number of years I have been teaching?" Dwarka Das was puzzled. It was really a brain-racker. He kept on thinking over the problem.

Well, would you not like to help Dwarka Das? Then come on. Tell the number of years the Masterji had been teaching. Also tell the ages of all the three.

■■

Seth Chandrika Mohan had six sons — Chandra Mohan, Tejander Mohan, Pankaj Mohan, Ramesh Mohan, Ram Mohan and Shyam Mohan.

Before retiring to Vanprastha Sethiji wanted to assess the ability of each his sons to manage his

Exactly after one month all the six sons gathered together. They had put their money in different trades. The total profit of all the sons amounted to Rs. 5600. The eldest son Ram Mohan earned Rs. 100 as profit whereas the youngest son Chandra Mohan's profit was Rs. 300. The remaining

business. His aim was to choose the best one.

In order to test them, Chandrika Mohan called his sons and gave money to each of his sons to invest in a business of his choice. He told them that he would assess their achievements after a month.

He had not given an equal amount of money to each of his sons. He gave Rs. 100 to his eldest son. Rs.200 to No.2, Rs. 300 to No. 3, Rs. 400 to No.4, Rs.500 to No. 5, and Rs. 600 to his 6th son.

sons Tejander Mohan, Shyam Mohan, Pankaj Mohan and Ramesh Mohan had earned profit to the tune of 2 times, 3 times, 4 times and 5 times respectively of the given capitals.

At the end, Seth Chandrika Mohan appointed his 4th son, who had done cloth business as the successor to his business.

Can you assess the amount of profit earned by each of his sons in their trade. Whether Sethiji was right to appoint his fourth son as his successor to the business. ■■

The Capital Water Supply Corporation had constructed a huge water tank behind Rashtriya Adarsh Vidyalya. This was the highest and biggest water tank in the Capital. The square-root of its capacity, when represented in litres, would stand in four digits. The last four digits of the capacity represented the square of a certain figure.

Coincidentally if these four digits were removed, the remaining number would be equal to the total number of students in the school.

Now, would you tell the capacity of this huge tank in litres? We may give you a lead—the water capacity of this tank was in tens of millions of litres.

■■

School

The spies of 'Dushta Nagar', wanted to destroy the water supply system of their neighbour state of Ram Nagar.

They gathered the information in order to carry out their plan. The water tank was stationed on the bank of a river flowing by the border of Ram Nagar. The pipe supplying water to the city was so large that it could empty one fifteenth water of the tank in one hour. The water supply to the city was open for twenty-four hours, being the Capital. That is why the pipe was never closed. Apart from the main pipe, there were three additional pipes to supply water to the small tanks constructed at the three palaces, those of the King, the Prime Minister and the General.

The capacity of the two pipes leading to the Prime Minister's and General's tanks was half of the capacity of pipe leading to King's palace. When these three pipes were also opened they could empty the main tank within seven and a half hours. The outlet of water pipe of the King's palace was in lakhs of litres in one hour. This figure of litres had no odd number in it.

The capacity of this tank when measured in litres was in seven digits.

It is not known whether the spies were successful in their plan to destroy the water supply system. They were definitely not able to assess the outlet capacity of the pipe leading to the King's palace.

Can you tell how many litres of water was supplied to the King's palace in one hour?

■■

Het Ram is an errand-boy employed recently at Hotel Bharat. One day he had to go to a pier, collect a packet and run back to the lighthouse. The manager timed his run to and fro. Having run from his hotel to the pier in five minutes, Het Ram took another fifteen minutes to reach the lighthouse. The lighthouse is only twice as far from the hotel as the pier. What explanation is there for this, in view of the fact that Het Ram ran without pause, at the same constant pace and never deviated from the straight beach? ■■

In view of the increasing power cuts, Chowdhary Nathan Singh had provided four diesel generators to his factory. These were imported from Germany, England, Russia and Japan. They began to produce 300, 400, 600, 700 units of electricity per hour, respectively.

Last Friday there was complete power-failure, as a result of which all the four generators were switched on simultaneously at 1 o'clock. After 4 hours the first generator was switched off. The second was switched off 2 hours later. One hour after this the third generator went out of order and could not be re-started.

Two hours after this the electrical supply commenced and the fourth generator was switched off.

During all this time all the four generators had produced 13,700 units of electricity.

From the above can you tell which generator ran for how many hours and how many units of electricity did each produce? ■ ■

The Rogues at Large

44

Seva Das was going to Bombay. His friend Chatura Nand warned him to beware of one Danga Nath and his cronies living near Mahalakshmi Temple who fleece the travellers. They were not only cheats but also liars. But on the other hand Ram Nath and his servants were good people. They were also reliable and helpful to strangers.

When Seva Das reached Mahalakshmi Temple he met three persons, namely Ranjit, Dilip and Panthe. Seva Das remembered the warning given by Chatura Nand. He asked those people who were they?

Ranjit said he was an employee of Ram Nath and the remaining two persons were Danga Nath's men.

Ranjit spoke in an inaudible whisper. Seva Das could not make out what he had said. He, therefore, asked the second person to repeat what Ranjit had said and also asked him about himself.

The second person, Dilip, said that the first person had told him that he was Ram Nath's man and the remaining two were Danga Nath's men. About himself he said he was Ram Nath's servant.

The third person was Panthe. On being asked the same question he said that the second man was Danga Nath's associate whereas, "I am Ram Nath's servant".

Can you tell who was actually the servant of Ram Nath? Who could be relied upon by Seva Das? Give your reasons for your answer. ■■

57

Krishan Kumar Sharma, Chief Inspector, Border Customs Department, had received information through International Police that eight notorious smugglers, namely Jackie, Javed, Jeevan Das, Dina, Victor, Robert, Ajay and Inder were coming to India with their leader by a plane. They were carrying smuggled goods. According to available information

they were supposed to enter the country on Wednesday morning via North-East border. These smugglers were to deliver L.S.D., morphine, gold biscuits, heroin and diamonds in packets to different cities.

On receipt of this important information Inspector Sharma

contacted his senior officers immediately and with a platoon of special police he reached the place where the smugglers were likely to enter from.

As soon as the suspected plane carrying the smugglers entered the border, a helicopter of Indian Air Force chased it. Inspector Sharma who was seated in the helicopter directed the smugglers to surrender themselves and to turn their plane towards the nearest aerodrome. However, all the smugglers, before reaching the appointed place, jumped down with the help of parachutes. They carried their packets with them. It was imperative for them to catch hold of any available transport and to distribute the smuggled goods to scheduled places. Among the get-away vehicles they used were a large truck and a car.

Victor dealt in drugs only. He got down at the outskirts of a nearby city. From here he had to go to Madras. But he could not get any transport to reach the city.

Ajay became unconscious as soon as he landed. He was carried to a distant hospital, 30 miles away, by the villagers who had gathered there. He regained his consciousness very soon. He thanked those who escorted him, and started for Delhi.

Jeevan's accomplice Dina was arrested by the police who seized four packets of heroin from him. Their destination was not Bombay.

Gold biscuits were to be delivered at Agra.

When Javed was arrested, police recovered L.S.D. tablets from him. His companion did not reach at the desired destination by bus. The smuggler who had taken lift in a truck did not go to Calcutta. Jackie was caught with diamonds. His accomplice reached Bombay safely.

Robert's vehicle was a four wheeler. Inder had to take his goods to a steamer called 'Mantoor'. Those who used bus and bullock-carts were smugglers dealing in drugs.

Inspector Krishna Kumar could arrest only three smugglers. He was disappointed. Five smugglers managed to reach their scheduled destinations and their leader escaped in a helicopter which was waiting for him in a nearby jungle.

Can you tell:

(a) Which smuggler was to deliver which smuggled goods?

(b) What was his mode of transport, after alighting from the plane, to reach at a near by city?

(c) Who was the leader of the gang?

Lead: The leader's name could be formed by taking first letters from the names of those smugglers who had gone to Agra, Calcutta, Delhi, Bombay and Madras. ■■

Y ou are not called upon to test your skill in the game of cards. It is merely a colour problem.

Take a pack of playing cards. You know they are 52 in all. Separate the red from the black. Now give it to me, I have arranged them as under :

Pile No. 1: There are three times as many blacks as red.

Pile No. 2: There are three times as many reds as black.

Pile No. 3: There are twice as many blacks as red.

Now, could you tell number of cards of each colour in each of the three piles? ■■

Delhi Transport Corporation had started a two -rupee travel-as-you-please ticket during the Ninth Asian Games, which would permit a ticket-holder to travel in any bus and go around the capital.

On 1 December, Ranjit, a known miser, also purchased a two-rupee ticket. Now, since he had spent two rupees he wanted to make the maximum use of the ticket. That day, he took a 'Deluxe' bus to go to his office (Re. 1 fare), instead of ordinary bus as usual. This bus broke down enroute. He had, therefore, to take an ordinary bus (fare 30p.) to reach office.

In the evening after office hours he made some interesting trips as follows: (i) to Connaught Place – in de-luxe; (ii) from there to AIFACS Hall—in de-luxe; (iii) to Arya Samaj Road by *Laghu Mudrika* (normal fare, 50p.); (iv) to Azad Market, ordinary bus (normal fare 40p.) and finally back home by de-luxe.

Reaching home he found his wife ready to go to her parent's house. Ranjit was in possession of two-rupee ticket. So, he decided to accompany his wife and son Ravi. At the bus stand there were three buses ready; ordinary, *Laghu Mudrika* and de-luxe. Their fares, were: 40 p., 50 p. and Re 1 respectively.

All the three buses were to go to the same destination. Which bus would Ranjit Babu like to choose for all three passengers with a view to taking fullest advantage of the ticket he had paid for to save his money. ■■

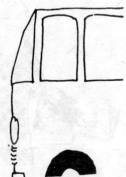

J agat Narayan had eleven sons. It was a 'happy eleven' and his friends would tease him with humour, "Hey, you have raised a full hockey team!"

But somehow, Jagat Narayan was not quite happy with life. It was all right to have many children and so many more pairs of hands to work in the field, but had he as much land! He had only eight and a three-fourth acres of land, not even one acre for each son.

One night, Jagat Narayan was taken ill suddenly and he passed away. He had not even prepared his will. All this befell so unexpectedly.

His sons divided the land amongst themselves. Each got an equal share, though small it was.

The peculiarity of the piece of land which came to the share of the youngest son Lakshaman, was that if he tied his cow in the middle of his field it could graze in every nook and corner of his field but it could not reach the other surrounding fields belonging to other brothers.

Lakshman required a 3-feet rope to tether his cow to the peg placed at the centre, as also to tie it round the cow's neck.

What should be the total length of the rope? ■■

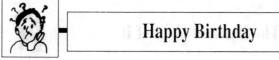
Year : 1991

Nearly two years and a little more from today, Radha's neighbour Alka asked her what her age was on her (i.e. Radha's) last birthday?

Radha replied that she was 12 years old.

"And how old would you be on your next birthday?"

Radha replied, "Aunty, if I do not fail in any class I shall be completing 12 + 3 course and would be studying for my M.A. on my next birthday."

Alka was puzzled.

Could you tell the exact date, month and year on which Alka had asked Radha the above question?

The Kendriya Sachivalaya Hindi Parishad is an establishment that propagates the use of Hindi in the Government of India's offices and other institutions under it. The Delhi branch holds elections of its executive council every year. Representatives from all branches in all over the country participate in the elections. In these elections only the central representatives can support and vote. As per the rules they elect President, Vice-President and twenty two other executive members. The President, in turn, selects in consultation with the Vice-President, eight secretaries besides one each for management, office administration and organisation, etc.

Satish Kumar Sethi was coming to Delhi much before the elections as a representative of his bank. It was a long journey. Tired, he fell asleep during it and being pre-occupied, in his mind, with the elections he dreamt of it. In the dream he saw elections being held. Some of the representatives, who were proposed more than once were declared elected by raising of hands.

Suddenly the train stopped with a jerk and Satish woke-up.

In his dream Satish had seen four representatives being elected. He could remember only some of the important events of this election.

On the basis of following data, tell who suggested whose name for which post and who supported him? How many votes did he get?

Four contesters, viz. Shri

Ashish Banerjee, Dr Bhaskar Rai, Bhimbali Verma and Shivchandra Saxena secured 30 more votes than the three and a quarter times of the total of present representatives. Maximum votes were secured by the President who got all the votes except 15.

Two other successful candidates had the difference of 18 votes. The fourth contester secured 2/3rd of the votes got by the President but this figure was not 252. Two out of these contesters were appointed as management secretary and organising secretary. The contesters who was seconded by Mayadin was not proposed by Ganga Prasad. Ganga Prasad's candidate secured less votes than other three contesters. Candidate supported by Satish got more votes than others. Bhimbali Verma secured more votes than Shivchandra but he was not elected as President.

The candidate supported by Shri Puttu Lal Gupta got third place on the basis of votes cast.

Rishiram Goyal proposed the name of a candidate for the post of President who got more votes than the candidate proposed by Bhola Nath. Dr Bhashkar Rai was supported by Shri Darshan Lal but Dr Rai was not the management secretary.

Shri Mayadin had proposed one of the candidates. The total number of central representatives was such that after dividing them in the groups of 2 to 7 no candidate will remain aloof. ■■

The enemy attacked suddenly on the Western border. The Chief of the Army Staff successfully countered the attack and gave the enemy a befitting reply.

In order to forestall any future move by the enemy, he made arrangements to obtain special type of equipment. There was a railway line running from the Western border to the Capital via Domrer and Kansaru.

Loaded with the necessary equipment, a special train with 40 wagons reached Domrer immediately. The second special goods train which had 45 wagons started after three days with other equipment. The day this second train started from the Capital, the first train had already been unloaded and it was to return to the Capital after unloading. When the second train started for Kansaru from Dumbrali, the empty train left Domrer for Kansaru, just a little later. No sooner these two trains were in the vicinity of Kansaru, than the enemy started bombing. Their target was Domrer station and the military establishments. But the bombs missed their targets and destroyed the third siding line at Kansaru station (as shown in the picture). As a result of this the siding line could not be used for trains. Immediately after the bombing was over both the trains were approaching to reach Kansaru railway station, is one another's opposite direction. Since, on the remaining two lines, only 600 hundred feet of railway track was left on the first main line, and 660 feet of track was left on the second line adjoining to the platform; it was impossible to allow both the

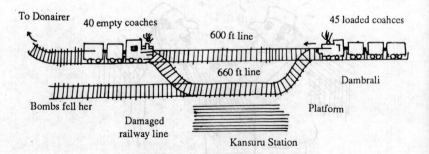

To Donairer · 40 empty coaches · 600 ft line · 45 loaded coahces · 660 ft line · Dambrali · Bombs fell her · Platform · Damaged railway line · Kansuru Station

trains to cross each other. The length of each wagon of both the trains was 30 feet and the length of each engine was 50 feet.

It was not possible for any of the two trains to take reverse journey. Every moment was precious. There was danger of bombing also at any moment. Station Master Rajpal was in a quandary. He did not know what to do. At this juncture retired Station Master Haridas reached the railway station. Rajpal explained to him his problem.

Haridas told Rajpal the trick by which both the trains could pass and according to his advice the trains started for their destination.

Can you guess how the two trains had passed? ■■

Randhir and Baldeo were good friends. Both were proud of their rides: Randhir of his scooter and Baldeo of his horse.

Each boasted that his was the fastest means of riding. And one day they decided to bet on it. They were to race on a road around a nearby lake which was at some distance from the village. They were required to take a full round of that road. The first to reach the starting point was to be that road. The road around the lake was circular. This road was 35 feet broad and 22 feet length in its circumference.

On the appointed day Randhir generously offered Baldeo 16 minutes handicap which the latter gleefully accepted. Baldeo cleverly positioned his horse at the road-end towards the lake. Baldeo kicked his horse exactly at 12:10 a.m., whereas Randhir started his scooter 16 minutes later, i.e. at 12:26 a.m.

Baldeo won the race by 30 seconds despite the fact that the average speed of his horse was less by 6.4 km. per hour than the Randhi's scooter. Randhir had to eat an humble pie.

Can you tell: (a) Average speed of Randhir's scooter, (b) How much distance did he cover?

■■

Mange Lal was often absent-minded. One day he went to the bank to withdraw some money but forgot the exact amount he wanted to withdraw, with the result that he inter-changed rupees and paise he required.

On his way back home he made some purchases: mangoes for Rs. 10.40; 1 kg soap for Rs. 7; two toys worth Rs. 3 each were bought by him for Rs. 2 each. On reaching home he saw that the balance amount left with him after the above purchases was double the amount he wanted to withdraw.

Now, you are required to assess the amount Mange Lal had written on his cheque. ■■

F ive young men, namely Jacob, Daljeet, Balbir, Safdar and Sudarshan entered the Indian Navy, about 30 years ago. In the final examination after the training period they were the foremost amongst the successful candidates. They secured the first five positions.

One of them was promoted to the rank of Vice-Admiral. The remaining four were holding the following ranks:

Rear Admiral, Commodore, Captain and Commander.

They had taken their training in I.N.S. 'Kashmir', 'Delhi', 'Dhavalgiri', 'Nilgiri' and 'Mysore'.

From the details given below you have to tell which youth was trained on which ship, which place did he obtain merit-wise and which was the last rank to which he had been promoted.

Note: These five did not get their present ranks on the basis of their seniority in the merit list.

The cadet on 'Kashmir' had secured the first place and he was senior to Sudarshan in rank.

The cadet on 'Delhi' was Daljeet. He obtained second place.

The trainee on 'Nilgiri' stood fourth but this cadet was not Jacob. The trainee on 'Dhavalgiri', Balbir was Commander. Next to Daljeet in seniority was Safdar who could never supersede Baljeet.
■■

Ranjit Kumar was called 'Lattoo' by his friends because of his habit of twisting the facts.

This incident relates to the year 1981. One day when his friend Krishan Dutt asked him about the date of his marriage, he told that he did not remember the date but when he was married, his wife was younger to him. Exactly on the day of second anniversary of his marriage his son Randhir was born.

He added, "Today Randhir is as old as his mother was at the time of her marriage".

"When Randhir would be half my age his mother's age would be 1/8th more than double the age of what she was at the time of our marriage. One thing more, when we celebrated Randhir's third birthday my wife was as old as I was at the time of our marriage."

What 'Lattooji' had said went over the head of Krishan Dutt. Can you tell in which year Lattoo was married? ■■

Rajiv had sent a clock for his father Sant Kumar from Kuwait. There was a peculiarity in this battery operated clock. It was like this:

A cuckoo used to come out of the clock to announce the time. It would coo as many times as the exact hour. After every 15 minutes the bird would coo only once. In addition to this the clock had in its middle bulbs of different colours, namely red, blue, yellow, green and sky blue. These bulbs would sparkle when the bird cooed and would extinguish when it stopped cooing. Although these bulbs flashed pale light yet their sparkling was extremely attractive.

Sant Kumar had lovingly hung this clock on a wall in his bedroom. Last night when all were fast asleep Sant Kumar heard a gun-shot from a neighbouring house. One minute later, Sant Kumar heard the cooing of the bird and simultaneously saw the sparkling of the bulbs once only.

Sant Kumar thought the nearby house was attacked by dacoits. He immediately came out in his balcony. While coming out he did not forget to carry with him his double barrel gun. It was a moonlit night. The stars were twinkling in the sky. Except for the barkings of a dog or two, he heard nothing and saw no movement anywhere. Af-

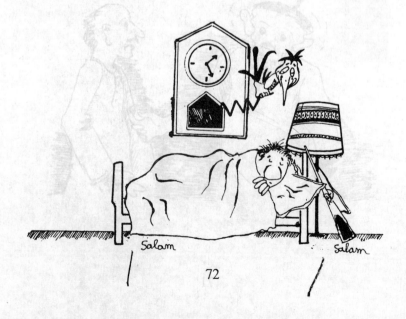

Salam

Salam

ter 2 or 4 minutes he came back into the house.

He wanted to know the time. As he groped for the switch he found that there was no electricity and hence he could not switch on the bulb. Being a non-smoker he had no match box with him and could not produce a temporary light also. He was in a fix. At that time the cuckoo cooed and all the five bulbs sparkled, but he could not see the hands of the watch in the light of the bulbs. At this juncture he had an idea. He kept himself awake.

After sometime he could know when the bullet was fired and what was the exact time. Then he went to sleep.

Can you say how long did he keep awaking maximum and minimum? And during the time when he was awoken maximum, what was the time when the gun-shot was fired? ■■

Three 'poker-face' pokers, namely Jamal, Billu and Tahir were poking fun at each other.

They started the game with funds in their pockets as under:

1. Tahir and Billu had together three times as much as Jamal.

2. Jamal and Billu had four times as much money as Tahir.

3. In the evening they finished their game and the position was—Jamal and Billu had three times as much as Tahir.

Tahir and Billu together had twice as much as Jamal. Billu finished with Rs. 2/-.

Now, without using your mathematical knowledge would you tell how much money did each of the three, pockers finished within his vallet?

■ ■

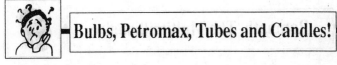
Padampur was a small township like any other village with an average population. When electricity was being supplied to the village most of the people got their connections.

Nevertheless, there were yet some houses using petromax or ordinary lamps for want of electric connections. Their proportion was as follows: The houses using lamps only were 20 less than the square of the exact number of houses using petromax, whereas houses using both, gas (petromax) and lamps were half the number of houses using only gas (i.e. petromax).

Those who had obtained electric connections were using tubes or bulbs as per their income. Those with only tubes were thrice in number of those with only petromax and the number of only bulb users was 2/3 of the square of only tube users. Now, those who had both bulbs and tubes were 1 more than twice the number of those using only petromax.

There was one house which had all the three, i.e. tube, petromax and lamp. Those using petromax, tube and bulb were 4 times the square of those houses which had all four means of illumination. The number of houses using bulb and petromax was equal to the number of houses using bulb, petromax, lamp plus the number of houses using bulb, petromax, lamp and tube.

Only two houses had lamps and tubes. 130 houses had bulbs and lamps and three houses had all the three, i.e. tube, bulb and lamp.

There was no house that was not covered by lighting arrangements detailed above.

If a three-digit figure of equal number is added to the number of houses in the township, the total would be exactly 1000.

Can you tell the number of houses that existed in Padampur?

It may be noted that the number of only gas users was in two digits.

Please also enlighten about number of houses (a) using tubes, (b) using bulbs, (c) using gas (petromax), and (d) using lamps.

■■

It was only last year that Ramnath had purchased a huge building in the New Market area for Rs. 25 lacs. Ramnath had become a millionaire in no time and now he aspired to become a multi-millionaire.

Not long before, he was just an hawker selling cloth from village to village. He could not ascertain positively how long ago it was, but the square root of the number of these years forms a complete figure.

The number of the house in which Ramnath lived in those days was in four digits. It was rather interesting that although not a very bright student of mathematics in his school days, he was able to remember only the square-root of his house number, rather than the number of the house.

Further, if we prefix his house number by the square of those years, the figure arrived at would be equal to the capital he owned at the time of finalization of accounts, last year.

Would you calculate his last year's capital?

To guide you a little further, I may add that he had often given to his son money equal to the square-root of his capital in one-rupee notes. And his last year's capital also contains figure 5 somewhere. ■■

Rameshwar Das was all alone in a railway compartment. He was wishing for some company. After all it was a long journey and would be boring with no one to talk to. Luckily, two passengers did board his compartment at the next stop. Their sundry conversation revealed that one of them was Balram and the other was Ghanshyam. Rameshwar did not much like indulging in coversations with strangers, so he just listened quietly to their talks which ran thus:

"Ghanshyam, I have now crossed sixty. And, as you know my only son Ravindra was married when he had completed 25. And do you know, it is our birthday today. Is not it a coincidence".

"Ya! indeed, it is," said Ghanshyam.

Balram further explained that his son Ravindra was half his age that very day.

"I hope, you remember Ghanshyam that 5 years ago when I had not reached sixty, I used to carry my grandson on my shoulders and roam about. Did not I do so?" Balram further said, "Yes, you did so." Ghunshyam nodded.

"Some years ago, when I was celebrating his birthday, I was just double his age. Can you guess how many years back this could have happened?" Balram further added.

Ghanshyam pondered. Rameshwar Das was also won-

dering how many years back this could have happened.

The train pulled up at a station and both friends got down. Rameshwar could not solve the puzzle. Would you help Rameshwar? Also tell the ages of Balram and his son on that particular day. ■■

Avinash took great interest in solving new mathematical problems. After forming problems and then solving them he used to show them to his friends. One day having formulated a problem he gave it to a friend to solve it. His friend could not solve the same even after great efforts.

Would you try it?
Here it is (see figure below)
Hint : $B^2 - A^2 = A + B$.

$$
\begin{array}{r}
7\,a - b \\
a\ \overline{\big)\ =\ =\ -\ -\ -\ -} \\
\end{array}
$$

(Hint: $b^2 - a^2 = a+b$)

Every individual dreams of having his own house. With a view to providing a house to the retired Government servants and also for those who would be retiring soon, Town Development Corporation had 'made a plan.

Priority-wise the plan was as under: (i) Every person retiring within three years after 3 March, 1983; (ii) Those who would be retiring 3 years before 3 March, 1983; (iii) Those who have already retired before three years since 3 March, 1983.

Amount to be deposited as advance by those desirous of having a house was as under:

(a) Low Income Group – Rs. 2500.

(b) Middle Income Group – Rs. 5000.

(c) High Income Group Rs. 7500.

Now, Subedar Balbir Singh who was rewarded Rs. 8000 by Lord Cornwallis for arresting some thieves while he was unarmed, desired to have a house under Middle Income Group.

Which priority would he be considered entitled for by Town Development Corporation? ■■

63 — Income Tax Raids

Seth Jamna Das Rangwale's business concerns were raided by Income Tax Officer Veerendra Kumar on the basis of information, by an informer of the department. Under the strict supervision of the Police Force, the I.T. officials ransacked the bungalow and the office of Seth Jamnadas, thoroughly. But they found nothing there. Disappointed, Veerendra Kumar was about to retreat along with his men when Seth Jamna Das's diary was discovered. The diary revealed lots of names and addresses but none of them had anything to do with the suspicious matter on hand. Deep Chandra Verma, an Inspector of the department, while replacing the diary picked up a piece of paper that had slipped out of the diary. The paper had some details recorded on it. (See details given below). Surendra Tripathi, another Inspector, on going through these details was extremely glad. He knew that the paper in question would reveal the underhand business. But the information on that paper was not easy to decipher. While all of them were in suspended animation an old and experienced officer of the I.T. Department came to their rescue and read out the contents.

Would you tell from the inscription below— the amount to be claimed by Sethji individually and the names of the people involved.

See details below : ■■

Dineshwale	L K Z X T L K / K X
Rameshji	A L X L C B K / K X
Shambhu Nath	J Y X A L J K / K X
Banwari Lal	K T Z E B T K / K X
	Z Y Z A E E J / J X

King Chatursen, as a reward, gave a triangular piece of land to his poet Veerdev. All the three sides of this land measured $150^2/_3$ yards, $195^3/_4$ yards and 45 yards 3 inches respectively. The happy poet reached home. His wife had been long asking him to have a piece of land where she could have built a home, a garden and finally a temple in each corner.

The poet with all elation told his wife of the reward he had secured from the king. But he was surprised not to see his wife happy. His wife said something which could not be heard. Then, can you tell why was his wife not happy and what did she said to her poet husband. ■■

The popular cine-star Shalini was found dead in her room in the famous hotel Sarva-Priya, on the New Year's day, i.e. the first of January. She had come here to discuss matters relating to shooting of her new film. Preliminary enquiry revealed that it was a case of murder.

The mode of murder suggested that the criminal had stabbed her with a knife and that he was a lefthander.

The news of her cruel murder spread chaos in the city. On 10 January 1981, C.I.D. Chief, Krishna Datt Sharma had arrested four infamous criminals in this connection with the help of his colleagues. They were: Karim alias Barchi, Bishna alias Jaki alias Qatar alias Hawai, D'Souza Jani and Premswaroop Captain. All the four were lefthanders, declared criminals and had undergone long term imprisonments. They were known for cruelty and had never admitted their crimes. But Krishna Datta Sharma had his own ways of investigations. After some interrogation he began questioning each suspect separately. He had used all 'police methods' of investigations and obtained the following statements:

Bishna : "I did not murder Shalini, Karim and Premswaroop Captain are close friends. I do not know who committed the crime".

Karim : "I have not killed Shalini.

I knew her well. I do not know Premswaroop Captain".

D' Souza Jani : "I have not committed this crime. Karim had told me that he had lived with Bishna for four days from 31 December. This crime is committed by Bishna."

Premswaroop Captain : "I have not killed Shalini. Bishna, Karim and I had been living together from 31 December 1980, to 3 January 1981 and had not separated for a moment. Karim has not committed this crime".

Krishna Datt Sharma came to the conclusion that the murderer was one of these suspects. Each one's statement had only one sentence which was wrong or false. He arrested the actual criminal after studying these statements minutely.

Could you guess who was Shalini's actual murderer? Why do you think so? State in brief.

■■

Fauja Singh, the grand-father of Shamsher Singh had captured four spies of Hitler's Nazy army. It was after some years that he was rewarded for this act of bravery with Rs. 5000 in cash and a special medal.

At the time of the receipt of the reward, Fauja Singh's age plus the age of his son Jarnail Singh, was half the age of Shamsher Singh plus the age of Fauja Singh, as would be on 30 March 1972.

Ten years thereafter, i.e. in the year 1982, Shamsher Singh's age was 1/4 of his grand father's age, while his father Jarnail Singh's age was 8 years less than three times of Shamsher Singh's age.

Can you tell what was the ages of all the three in 1983? ■■

Compilation of a dictionary is not an easy task. It needs great efforts, accuracy and meticulous care. Nevertheless, Prof Shyam Nath accepted the challenge and brought out a huge dictionary just within four years and entitled it *Bhaskar Kosh*. The entries of words, their definitions and meanings made the book worth more than ten lacs words.

Bhaskar Kosh had 62, 623 words more than *Diwakar Kosh* compiled by Prof Diwakar. The latter contained more than nine lacs words. Interestingly, the number of words in *Diwakar Kosh* did not contain figure 4 nor did any figure appear twice.

The number of pages of *Diwakar Kosh* was equal to 6 more than double the square root of number of words + 522.

Would you calculate : (a) Total No. of words in *Bhaskar Kosh* of Prof Shyam Nath? (b) Total number of pages in Diwakar's *Diwakar-Kosh*? ∎∎

Surajmals' factory was located a little away from the capital. The place had no Air Service. So Surajmal had to take flight up to Delhi and then travel by car to his factory which took him 3 hours.

Surajmal used to take flight 0040 of Pawan Doot from Calcutta to Delhi. This was a very punctual service. At the dot of 5.30 a.m., flight 0040 used to deplane passangers. After completing the airport formalities within ten minutes, Surajmal would be in his car and off would he go instantly.

Once Surajmal had to visit his factory urgently. Since the plan was made at the eleventh hour, he could not get his ticket for his usual 0040 flight. Instead, he took flight 0036 and landed at the airport in the early morning hours, i.e.

3:20 a.m. His manager Janak Ram informed him on telephone that his car had left for the airport on time but may not have arrived due to flood. The entire area was flooded and vehicular traffic was disturbed.

En route there was a bridge. It was difficult for any motor vehicle to cross the bridge against the force of flood-water. While he was pondering over the situation, Surajmal remembered that one of his employee's father resided in a village nearby. When he reached the village, he was greeted by Ram Prasad, father of Jeevan Lal. Ram Prasad suggested that he could help Surajmal to cross the bridge in his bullock-cart, Surajmal agreed and at 4:10 a.m. the cart started. By the time Surajmal reached the place

Car picks up
Surajmal from here

where he used to board his car, 60 minutes had lapsed between that time and alighting from the plane.

The car was coming towards the bridge at the same average speed at which it used to take Surajmal from the airport to his factory. The cart crossed the bridge and at the same time the car pulled up at the spot. Surajmal wanted to give Ram Prasad some money for the obligation but the latter refused to accept.

Surajmal was in a hurry and he immediately started for the fac-tory. It took just five minutes for him to get down from the cart and to get into the car. The car was going back at the same speed at which it had come. Despite Surajmal's apprehensions the car reached the factory 15 minutes earlier than usual.

Ram Prasad's bullock-cart had run at 10 km/p/h.

Can you tell the average speed of car? What was the distance between the airport and his factory? How many kilometres had the bullock-cart covered? ▪▪

Chandra Prakash was travelling in Ahmedabad Express. While he was sleeping, Jamnagar Mail from opposite direction crossed his train at a great speed. The noise made by the Mail train woke Chandra Prakash. He sat up still half-asleep. He began to look around. His co-passangers were talking. Chandra also listened to them.

"Shyam, the Jamnagar Mail was going at a great speed, don't you think so?"

"Indeed, Dev Kaka! It crossed our train just in a matter of seconds. What do you think the speed was?" Shyam asked.

Dev Kaka replied, "Yes, the speed was considerably great. But our train too is running at much speed. Ahmedabad Express, as you know, is less than one thousand feet but is longer than the Jamnagar Mail by 150 feet. Besides, the mail had diesel engine."

"Yes uncle, but I couldn't find out the speed."

Chandra Prakash who was listening to this conversation intervened and said that if he knew the time taken by these trains to cross each other and their total length, he would be able to tell the speed of the Jamnagar Mail.

Dev Kaka offered the following details: "The average speed of the Jamnagar Mail is so much more than the Express that it could have crossed the Express in one minute. Both the trains were running at a speed that was in whole numbers in miles. If they came from opposite directions they would pass each other in 10 seconds. I have never measured their total length, but definitely it is not less than 550 yards."

Now tell the average speed and length of both the trains. ■■

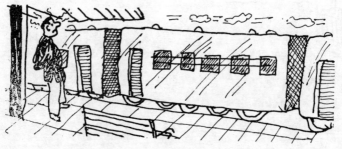

Representatives from all states had come in groups to the capital to participate in the Republic Day Parade. Most of the states had sent their tableaux. The producers of the tableaux had been awarded according to the standard. The artists who received 1st, 2nd, 3rd, special and consolation prizes belonged to Assam, Kerala, Gujarat, Punjab and Haryana, respectively. The names of the producers were Kashmiri Lal Gupta, Gafoor Khan, Prem Da, Michael D'sauza and Raghuveer Singh. From the following details would you tell : Which state had brought which tableau? Who was its producer? Which award was he given?

The tableau, 'The army on the front' received the consolation prize. Its producer was Prem Da.

The second prize was awarded to Gafoor Khan but it was not for the tableau, 'The bungalow of flowers'.

'Village life' was awarded the third prize. It was a tableau from North India.

Kashmiri Lal Gupta had produced, 'The farmer and the harvest' but this tableau did not represent Southern or Eastern states.

The prize awarded to Haryana was not special prize. Michael's tableau belonged to a state which was situated on seashore but he too did not receive the special prize. A South Indian state had shown, 'A tea estate'. The 'Bungalow of Flowers' did not come from any Eastern state.

■■

Colonel Sita Ram had ordered 25 seedlings of gauva for planting them in his orchard. He directed his gardener Ganga Ram to plant these seedlings in 22 rows in such a way that each row should have five plants in a straight line. Ganga Ram did not know how to do it. Will you help him?

It is quite sometime since Ram Prasad has been running a tailoring shop. He did not do well in the beginning. Incidentally, one day he came across a saint who told him that triangular articles would prove lucky for him. Accordingly, Ram Prasad gave a triangular shape to his shop. It is difficult to say whether it was a matter of sheer chance or pure luck, but the fact remains that his business began to flourish. Next he got made for himself an iron scale to measure cloth, also in a triangular shape and marked it with inches so as to facilitate cutting of cloth from one inch to one yard without any difficulty.

The news of Ram Prasad's success spread and his neighbour, Shyam Chandra, the proprietor of Shyam and Sons Tailors, also decided to get a similar triangular measuring plate made for himself. He somehow managed to obtain the details of the shape of Ram Prasad's plate and got one iron plate (as shown in the figure) made for himself.

Now, the problem was to mark the plate with 1 inch to 1 yard markings so that Shyam Chandra could, without difficulty, measure any cloth at a stretch.

Can you help Shyam

Chandra?

Note :

(i) Shyam Chandra should be able to measure a cloth of any length from an inch to one yard at one time.

(ii) It is important that the number of marking should be in minimum figures.

(iii) While taking measurements the cloth in question is required to be wound round the measuring plate as is done by cloth merchants while measuring cloth by their measuring rods.

Seth Girdhari Lal had purchased an imported 'Show-piece' in Bombay. The height of the piece was 3 yards and $6\frac{1}{2}$ inches and the thickness was 2 inches. He was to travel by train from Bombay to Delhi.

However, he received information that his son Satyendra had taken ill, so he could no longer stay in Bombay and decided to travel by air.

Sethji wanted to take the show-piece along with him. But the authorities would not allow the show-piece by plane as according to their rules nothing beyond two yards in height was permissible to be carried along with a passenger. Sethji liked the piece immensely and would not leave it behind. Indeed, he faced a problem. After much thinking and planning, Sethji hit upon a plan and managed to bring the piece along with him in the plane.

Can you tell how was the show-piece brought? ■■

Pravin and mathematics were at daggers drawn. Pravin's father Sohan Lal was much disturbed. He wanted Pravin to be an expert mathematician but did not know ways and means to fulfil his ambition. At last he told his younger brother Madan Lal his problem.

Madan Lal assured him that he would try his best to see that Pravin becomes an expert in the subject. In order to achieve his objective he drew a hexagon on a piece of paper. He also drew another hexagon above it. Then in the middle of these a circle was drawn. Small circles were also drawn at the corner of these hexagons and also on the circumference of the inner circle. Some figures were written in a small circle and some were kept blank (see figure). Then, he asked Pravin to fill in the blank circles.

It took two days for Pravin to complete his assignment, nevertheless, he completed them successfully.

Will you tell what figures were written by Pravin in the circles concerned? It is not necessary to tell all the figures separately. It is enough to tell the total of figures in eighteen small circles. ■■

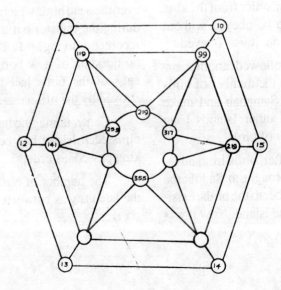

Nagaj Sen was the king of Nayabirirk group of Islands. His kingdom consisted of six Islands, namely Kamaij, Samahab, Sadobarba, Dad, Gobaito and Nagua. Nagaj Sen was good at heart and he often tried to please his subjects. But, because of his defective and faulty planning his subjects were not happy.

One day he had a 'Mohammd Tugahlaq' wave in his brain and he ordered that total birds from all the Islands be sent to Kamaij Island'. The number of birds to be sent from other Islands should be equal to the number existing in Kamaij at that time.

It was an order from the king and it had to be obeyed without reasoning. And, it was obeyed.

Then followed another order. Increase the number of birds six times at Samahab and make sure that all other Islands have equal number of birds.

Thereafter, birds from all Islands were brought to Sadobarba equal in number to the birds, existing then in the Island. Now it was the turn of Dad, Gobaito and Nagua. It was observed during the transfer of birds that all the six Islands had equal number of birds. The officials, however, counted even the dead birds which had died during the transfer but they were recorded as living birds. There was no question of new borns as the eggs of the birds had been destroyed by the officials.

Can you imagine how many birds each Island had before the king passed his orders?

The number of birds, on all the Islands was between five and six lacs. ■■

Cases of forgery in Banks had been on the increase during the past few days and the Banks had been directed to take remedial measures. 'Udyog Nagar' Banks held a meeting and took some decisions. The staff was directed to check all relevant aspects of cheques carefully at the time of cash payments against cheques. Payments were to be made only when the official was fully satisfied that the cheque/cheques were genuine.

Only ten days after this meeting, i.e. on 12 October, two customers came to 'Adarsh Rashtriya Bank', and presented a cheque to Shree Laxmimal official manning the counter. Laxmimal saw the cheque, asked the customer to sign on the back of the cheque and issued him a token after noting its number on the back of the cheque.

While sending the cheque to the cashier for payment, Laxmimal became suspicious and went to his officer. After discussing the matter, Laxmimal approached the Manager. From there he contacted the person on phone who had issued the cheque. It was confirmed that Laxmimal's suspicion was correct.

Now it was time to take action. Here, Laxmimal acted shrewdly. On his instance Radha Kishan, the teller, called the man who had presented the cheque and told him since the amount to be paid was large, he should come in and collect the money.

The Adarsh Rashtriya Bank Ltd.

UDYOG
NAGAR

18 - 8 1987

PAY _ Sunil Kumar

रुपये RUPEES   Eighty five thousand only.

या धारक को OR BEARER

भता गर्ने ₹.Rs 85000/-

खा. सं
A/c No.   बं प   इ नि
                      INTLS

The police was informed in the meantime and Inspector Devendra Singh arrived with his force. They arrested the forgers, on the spot.

Laxmimal was highly praised for his cleverness and timely action.

But what made Laxmimal suspicious about the cheque?

Mukesh purchased eight balls of the same weight, size and colour and kept them in a bag. After some time his younger brother Rakesh Came home and put his ball in the same bag. This ball was similar to the ones which Mukesh had put in, but was not equal in weight to them. When Rakesh came for the ball after sometime, he insisted on having his own ball.

Now Mukesh faced a problem. He had to sort out Rakesh's ball. Then it occurred to him that he should use a weighing machine. So, he procured one from his friend Ramesh and started sorting Rakesh's ball.

Can you help Mukesh in finding the ball that belonged to Rakesh in minimum time? Also state whether his ball was lighter or heavier than Mukesh's balls?

Maharaja Sajjan Singh was the ruler of 'Khushal Gadh'. There was no sign of poverty in his realm. The subjects were happy. But, his neighbour King Durjan Singh of 'Irsha Puri' was jealous of the prosperity of 'Khushal Gadh'.

Immediately after the rainy season Durjan Singh attacked 'Khushal Gadh', captured most of its land and surrounded the fort of 'Khushal Gadh'. The fort of 'Khushal Gadh' was pentagonal in shape. Each side of the fort was 250 yards long.

All around the fort Durjan Singh arranged his forces strategically. Maharaja Sajjan Singh was a great mathematician. He understood the reason to the arrangement of enemy forces. Within two days, counter-arranging his own army, he attacked in such a manner that 250 of the enemy soldiers including 18 riders of the supply force were killed.

On the other hand Sajjan Singh lost just 20 infantry soldiers and 2 of his cavalry men.

From the figure given below can you assess the total number of soldiers in both the armies and number of soldiers that survived? It is imperative that number of cavalry soldiers and infantry soldiers is calculated separately.

■■

Map of the War-field

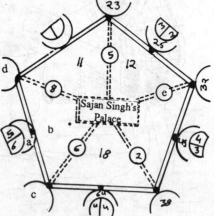

Note:
1. Sajjan Singh's soldiers: Cavalry-0, other members in the fort show infantry.
2. Durjan Singh's soldiers: Supply cavalry other members with fort show infantry.

N.C.C. cadets of Adarsh School were to be selected from among students of 10th class. Principal Shukla assigned this task to Head Master Sunder Lal, who was also the N.C.C. Captain. He selected 24 cadets out of 60 willing students from sections A,B,C & D. The names of the selected cadets were exhibited on the notice board. A naughty student who was not selected, tried to tear off the list. The list now showed 17 names. After the selection the Headmaster had gone out of station and as such it was difficult to trace out the name of remaining 7 students who were in the original list.

1. Zabermal, 2. Tikaram, 3. Tharousilal, 4. Bhagwan Singh, 5. Hari Singh, 6. Tanak Singh, 7. Bhagat Ram, 8. Chandan Singh, 9. Barkat Ali, 10. Zagadu Ram, 11. Samsher Singh, 12. Nazakat Hussain, 13. Thipa Ram, 14. Charlie, 15. Khemchandra, 16. Hussain Ali, 17. Himmat Singh.

The remaining seven names are contained in the following list:

1. Kamal Kumar, 2. Khairati Lal, 3. Ganpat Rai, 4. Ghananand, 5. Chandgi Ram, 6. Jwala Prasad, 7.Janakidas, 8. Zhandaram, 9. Thandi Ram, 10 Tanveer, 11. Dayanand, 12. Daroga Prasad, 13. Dhaniram, 14. Narayan Das, 15. Prem Singh, 16. Prakash Chand, 17. Fakir Chand, 18. Banarasi Das, 19. Bhim Singh 20. Madan Lal, 21. Yatindradas, 22. Ramesh Bahadur, 23. Lal Chandra, 24.Vakil Singh, 25. Sharad Chandra, 26. Satveer Singh, 27.Harinarayan Singh

Can you tell before the Head Master comes, the names of those lucky students, in serial order, that were in the list of selected candidates.

■■

Delhi Mail leaving from Bombay stopped at Palval Railway Station. After some time Hawrah Express came from Delhi and also stopped there.

Which of the trains, in your opinion, was at a longer distance from Delhi? ■■

From Bombay   Delhi Mail

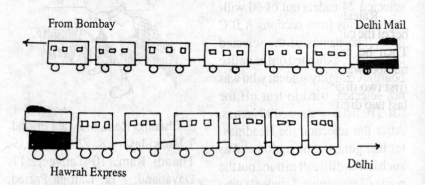

Hawrah Express   Delhi

When Ravi's Maruti car arrived, his younger brother Rajesh was eager to try it. Ravi handed over the key of the car to Rajesh and told him that the car was stationed at the parking place

Rajesh asked him the number of the car. Ravi began to laugh. Then he explained that the car number was rather attractive: "The first two digits are 1 less than the last two digits. No figure has been repeated. The value of the second digit is 2 more than the first. Now go and search and get going for a drive."

Rajesh should not have any difficulty in tracing the car. But the poor fellow went on searching without success.

Now it is up to you to help Rajesh. Hurry up and tell him the number of the car. ■■

Suresh Ratan was not too bad at remembering things but somehow he could never remember phone numbers. He used to forget the phone number even of his best friend Rajesh Sharad. He, therefore, jotted it down in his diary but unfortunately he misplaced the diary one day. Let us now try to help Suresh.

Delhi Telephones had opened some new centres recently. As a result of this, Rajesh's telephone number had changed from six digits to seven digits. The exchange code had come to 3 digits from 2 digits. The first number of the code remained the same. The second number was now 1 less than the previous second number. And the third number was 1 if the last four figures of the previous phone number went up to 5000 and if it was more than 5000, it would be 2.

It is significant to note that only the exchange code number had undergone a change in the revised phone number and that the last four digits remained the same. These last four digits of Rajesh's phone form a complete square. When 4 is added to the new exchange code number, it becomes a complete square and the full phone number including the exchange code number also becomes a complete square and this is an astonishing aspect of this telephone number.

Now, will you work out the new and old phone numbers of Rajesh!

◼◼

Paid Back

T he whole world condemned the war-mongering country when it attacked our peace loving one. Since mere condemnation was not sufficient for the aggressor to withdraw, some kind of counter-attack was necessary for self-defence.

The Air Force, therefore, went into action and under 'Operation Dhwansas' bombed the strategic places of the enemy including the capital, from their secret air-bases.

The following Air Force officers took part in this operation under Commander Balwant Singh: Ahmad Khan, E D'Souza, Raghuveer Pratap Singh, S. Subramaniam and Shrikant. These offices were: one Squadron Leader, one Wing Commander, two Flying Officers and two Pilot officers.

The bombers used for the these attacks included, Ajit, Canberra, Gnat, MIG-21 and Hunter. One officer used a helicopter the name of which was the same as of Maharana Pratap's horse.

These fighters deceived the four Sabre-jets and six Star fighters of the enemy, dodged their anti-aircraft guns, reached the targets in question and returned after bombing them.

While these bombers were returning, twelve highly sophisticated fighters of the enemy tried to surround them. But they were not successful. On the other hand two of the enemy war planes were de-

stroyed by our expert bombers. Not only this, they also damaged another two of the enemy's planes. One of our bombers was slightly damaged but all the bombers returned to their bases safely.

The first flight of this operation was started by Balwant Singh exactly at 8 a.m. One minute later the Gnat went into air, Ahmad Khan took-off at 8:02. It was this plane that had been damaged slightly during the return flight. Shrikant and Subramaniam were of the same rank. It was, however, Shrikant who started first.

E. D'Souza was not a flying officer but he was superior in rank to Khan. He started his bomber at 8:10.

The Hunter was manned by a flying officer and he took off one minute earlier than Ajit. The last flight took-off at 8:20. Ajit and the helicopter were piloted by the pilot officers.

This was the account of the attack on the war-mongering

country.

From the information supplied above and your knowledge of the Air Force, would you tell us: Name of the pilot and his rank, and the plane which he piloted? Also tell the timing of the flight. ■■

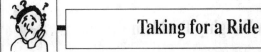
A bhinav was proud of his scooter so was Saurabh of his motor-cycle.

The number of Abhinav's scooter was a complete square of three digits. The peculiarity of this number was that if the first number of the scooter was placed at the last place it formed a full square and this full square formed the exact number of Saurabh's motor-cycle.

Can you tell the numbers of the scooter, the motor-cycle and their father's car?

It may seem to be very tricky problem. Well, we could tell you further clues to enable you to solve it. It is like this: If the number of the scooter and the number of the motor-cycle are added together you will obtain a figure of their father's car.

Various types of customers use to visit Lala Janakidas' shop. This involves weighing of things right from 1 kg to 364 kg usually. Lalaji desires to use the minimum number of weights. Would you be able to tell the number of weights and their weighing capacity which would enable Lalaji to weigh from 1 kg to 364 kg of goods with the help of minimum number of weights. ■■

Some important information leading to Sushila's murder was given by one Sudarshan Lal. He had cultivated a habit of noting in his diary the exact time of any strange, bizarre and unusual happening or event.

He had his way of recording time such as: If it was five minutes past seven, he would record 7:05. Or, when it was twenty minutes past one, it would be 1:20 in his diary.

That day too, he did the same. As soon as he saw two masked men entering a neighbouring house, he noted down the time. Two minutes later he heard six shots.

Later, it became known that those masked men had come to loot the house and when Sushila resisted one of them pressed the trigger and emptied the revolver on her.

The time noted by Sudarshan Lal would represent a figure in a complete square if the 'point' between hrs. and minutes were removed.

Another funny thing came to light. Had the reflection in the mirror of that particular time been noted and the decimal point removed, the figure would have represented two complete squares by the addition of 8 to it or subtracting 15 from it.

From the above, can you tell when the first bullet was fired?

■■·

aja Prem Singh of Khushal-garh was fed up with contin-ued attack on his kingdom by Raja Barbar Singh of Irshapuri. He, therefore, got a fort built in pentagonal form in Vishal Garh. It was a very big fort with each side measuring one and a half miles.

There were 20,000 residents in all, including the soldiers. Prem Singh deputed his oldest son Gulshan Kumar to look after the administration of the fort. The Yuvraj divided the fort in five sections. The soldiers in each section were stationed according to their strategic importance.

However, Barbar Singh was not the one to allow them peaceful existence. On a dark night, he made a massive attack on the Ajmeri Gate of the fort, with 10,000 soldiers. Ajmeri Gate was in section 1. Ram Gajraj Singh was the commander-in-charge. He called for troops from other sections— each section was to provide him with as many soldiers as section 1 had. 1200 soldiers of Barbar Singh's army were killed and 280 wounded. Gulshan Kumar, on the other hand, had 50 of his soldiers wounded. The next day Delhi Gate of the fort was attacked. This gate was in section 3. Commander Jagdish Chandra was in command of the troops here. He called for soldiers from all the other sections—each section to send as many troops as

were already present in this section. 30 of Gulshan Kumar's soldiers were wounded in this attack, whereas 855 of Barbar Singh's troops were killed and 200 wounded. This attack of Barbar Singh also proved futile. Barbar Singh attacked Jaipur Gate, Lahori Gate, and Fatehpur Gate, respectively but suffered heavy losses. Whichever section he attacked, it used to be reinforced by troops from other sections— each section sending as many troops as already present in the section under the attack.

It was to the credit of Gulshan Kumar's able leadership that none of his soldiers was killed during the operation. It is, however, true, that the gates fought for rendered 100,198 and 232 soldiers wounded, respectively. On the other hand Barbar Singh having had to fight in the open, suffered heavy casualities with 205, 309 and 1198 soldiers killed and 156, 319, 818 as wounded respectively.

A disappointed Barbar Singh returned to Irshapuri. Later, when the number of soldiers was accounted for, it was found to the astonishment of all, that they were equal in number in each section.

Can you tell how many soldiers were there in each section before and after the attack? ■■

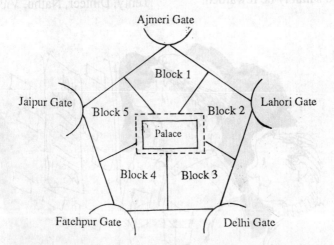

109

With a view to obtaining co-operation from the public and to create confidence in the minds of the people, the police launched 'Janta-Police-Co-operation' campaign, a few days ago. They had proclaimed their intentions by distributing hand bills, sticking posters on the walls and even making personal contacts with the public. In these attempts they had stressed the importance of police-public-contact in detecting crimes and apprehending the culprits. Further to enthuse confidence among the public, it was assured that action would be taken immediately on receiving information from it and the informer would suitably be rewarded.

All the posters and hand bills carried the names of Station House Officers along with their telephone numbers. It was not long before results of this campaign began to bear fruit. Jacobson, Pradyuman Kumar, Pritam Singh, Shish Ram and Suresh Chandra who were residents of different areas and conseioheir duty, informed their respective Station House Officers, namely Iqbal Jafar, Nafe Singh, Bhagwan Das, Ram Singh and Seva Ram through telephone numbers 43251, 262504, 311211, 371951 and 615973. On receipt of information police went quickly into action and arrested 5 proclaimed criminals, namely Tenty, Dinteer, Nathu, Vicky and

Singhada. The stolen property was also recovered from them.

From the information given above you are required to say: Which citizen gave information to which Station House Officer about which criminal? Also say which telephone number was used by that citizen?

Here is a lead which will help you in solving the problem—Jacobson had dialled 6 digits to contact Iqbal. Zafar was able to arrest the thief within two hours. He was taken before a magistrate where Tenty had already been produced. Tenty was not arrested either by Bhagwan Das or by Seva Ram. His informer was Pritam.

The informer who had got Vicky arrested had used the telephone with largest number. Pritam and Praduman did not use the number which could be divided by 2.

Ram Singh's phone number was less in digits than Nafe Singh's. Ram Singh had received information from Suresh which enabled him to arrest Dintir. Suresh had dialled 6 times.

The S.H.O. who arrested Nathu had phone number which could be divided by 2. The citizen's name who informed Seva Ram starts with letter P. ■■

111

Rajeshwar Nath had put most of his belongings in a blue trunk for use in his old age. He locked his trunk with a lock having a numerical device. He wanted to jot down these numbers in such a way that a reader may not be able to understand them. For this purpose he drew a figure of the shape resembling a cob-web and wrote some numbers in some of its columns.

Those figures, the total of which was equivalent to the number of his lock, were left blank,

cleverly.

But he himself forgot the number of his lock. He tried to fill in some numbers into the blank space but they would not make correct key numbers that might open the lock. In filling these he had made a small mistake somewhere.

Here is a lead for you to solve the puzzle:

Lead : All the four digits of the number of the lock are different.

■■

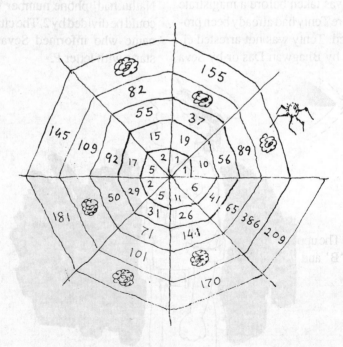

112

Shyam Chandra, the owner of Shyam and Sons Tailors, got a measuring plate made in a triangular shape. It exactly like the one which tailor master Ram Prasad had. This plate had four markings and could measure cloth from 1" to 36". Even this could not improve his fortune.

After some days he came across a famous saint who gave him an egg-shaped measuring plate, both sides of which measured 18" in length.

black and lower portion 'A', 'D', 'C' was white in colour. The white portion of the plate was marked in yellow colour indicating 1" to 1 yard, thus facilitating measurement in complete inches, of any cloth, at a stretch.

It was indeed a matter of coincidence that his business flourished considerably.

All this leaves me wondering just how many minimum marks the plate had and what was the

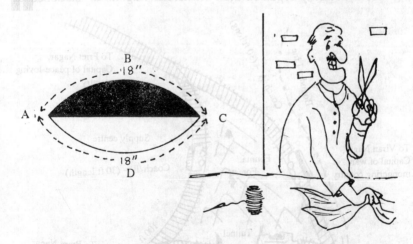

The upper portion of this plate 'A', 'B' and 'C' (see figure) was distance between two marks as also what figures they showed?

The army of a war-mongering country attacked the borders of a peace-loving country all of a sudden. The air force of war-mongering country had bombarded the Railway line that was between the two countries. This bombing destroyed the Railway line in such a manner that only 40 feet of line after Railway crossing 'B' was intact. In defence of the attack the peace-loving country positioned its troops immediately. After two days' fierce battle the peace-loving forces not only repulsed the attack of the enemy but also compelled them to be on the defence.

The movements of both the countries had slackened considerably which indicated that an all-powerful attack was in the offing.

The commander of the peace-loving country's forces took stock of the situation and found that wagon 'A' which was stationed at Preet Nagar-Viran Nagar line contained war equipment which were not required by the frontline forces whereas wagon 'B' stationed at

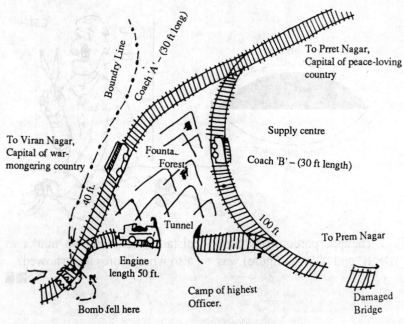

Preet Nagar-Prem Nagar line had ammunition which was required by the frontline forces immediately. Wagon 'B' had tank-destroying ammunition.

After studying the map the commander observed that there was an engine stationed in the tunnel 'E' at Prem Nagar-Viran Nagar line. He, therefore, issued order to inter-change the positions of the wagons with the help of the engine and send the engine back immediately into the tunnel. At this stage the commander was informed that the bridge towards Prem Nagar was destroyed during last night's bombing. Now, only 100 feet long Railway line could be used for movements. This piece of line was beyond Railway crossing 'D'.

The engine driver Ranchhod Das gave his opinion that it was not possible to interchange the two wagons, and even if the wagons were inter-changed it would be impossible for the engine to reach tunnel 'E' safely. So, he suggested that an engine should be requisitioned from Preet Nagar. Since it would take at least 10 hours for the engine to reach from Preet Nagar and since the anti-tank ammunition was required immediately, the Chief Commander consulted his officers.

At that moment he spotted a young officer with a broad smile and asked him the reason. In reply to it, Ashok Rai told his plan in detail to the driver. On hearing this the driver Ranchhod Das got up immediately and with long strides strode out of the room to inter-change the wagons. Could you tell about the plan which Ashok Rai told Ranchhod Das to inter-change the wagons and send the engine back into the tunnel 'E'?

■■

Now, we may have to go back to our school days to solve this drum problem.

One Mr Sita Ram was dealing in mobile oil. There were some big drums in his godown containing mobile oil and all the drums were of same size. His servant used to open the locked drums for issuing oil to the customers. One day the servant did not turn up and locks could not be opened for delivery. The customers arrived for oil. Sita Ram decided to make holes at the bottom and drain off oil for issue.

One servant Ramu drilled a 6 cm semi-circular hole in one drum. Another servant Khaldu drilled three holes of 5 cms each in another drum.

If the quantity of oil is the same in both the drums and if the oil is taken out from both the drums simultaneously, which drum would empty first? ▪▪

Geometry is sometimes a brain twister, too. But, this time it is not. Prem was doing his home work. With a radius of 20 cm he drew a circle. He then drew 7 lines inside the circle with the help of a foot-rule.

Can you tell in how many minimum and maximum divisions was the circle divided by these lines?

I t is not a thriller alone, it is a thrilling problem any way.

All this happened between Ghaziabad and Delhi. Dr Satish had a clinic at Ghaziabad. A person entered the clinic and collapsed on a sofa. The doctor ran to him and found that he suffered from a knife wound, quite deep and serious. It was bleeding profusely.

Enquiries revealed that he was Dr. Laxmi Prasad. He had come from Hapur carrying some important papers relating to "Atomic Energy and its uses in the field of peace and development works". Some anti-social elements had attacked him in trying to snatch away the documents. Laxmi Prasad did not care for his wounds nor for his life for that matter. All he wanted was to be escorted to Delhi after first aid with preliminary precautions. Dr Satish took him in his car, after necessary treatment, and the three — Dr Satish, Dr. Laxmi Prasad and the driver — left for Delhi.

Dr Satish observed that a truck bearing No. 3442 was following them. Dr Laxmi Prasad confirmed his doubt explaining that, that was the truck carrying the anti-social elements who had been following him and who had assaulted him.

The driver tried to dodge the truck by entering lanes and then drove towards Delhi.

At Delhi they found the truck again following them with utmost speed. While the distance between

the car and the truck was getting closer, the former entered Jamuna Bridge.

The distance between car and the 11th pole was one and a half times the distance between car and the 10th pole. Now, if the car were to move back in the reverse order towards entrance of the bridge from the present position, it would collide with the truck exactly at the entrance point.

The distance between the car and the truck was fast reducing.

If both vehicles maintained the same speed, the truck would smash the car from behind just at the exit end of the bridge. It was imperative for the car, therefore, to somehow cross the bridge to be able to escape any attack from the truck.

The bridge had 59 poles in all. Each pole was 25 metres apart. The first and the last poles were at a distance of 25 metres each from the banks of the river.

On reaching the middle of the bridge, the car doubled its speed. The truck came out of the last leg of the bridge immediately after the car.

The situation seemed tense. But Dr Satish met a police car before any untoward incident could take place. The police punctured the truck tyre with a pistol shot. And all was under control.

What was the speed of the car when it crossed the bridge? How far ahead was the car of the truck when the latter crossed the bridge?

■■

G yan Partrika a famous magazine known for its interesting stories and advertisements was very popular among its readers. Their 'New-Year' issue was full of variety and contained 89 advertisements. Among these advertisements 18 were quarter page size, 17 half page size, 18 full page (this includes 3 pages of the cover), 2 of two pages each, 1 of three pages and 1 of four pages. The remaining advertisers had included ads. in the advertisement panel. Each page of the panel advertisement had 8 ads.

The total number of pages allotted to the ads (including those on cover) were 39.67 per cent of the total pages of the magazine.

The pages containing poems were less by 20 than the pages covered by stories. The poetry portion was half a page less than a serialized novel by a popular writer. The illustrated story which was only one in number was two and a half parts of the novel. The short stories were three times more than the illustrated story. A humorous poem covered two pages, apart from it different poets had contributed 4 poems on four pages and 10 poems which were only 1/4th page length each. Remaining poems were half-page each.

Similarly, there were 5 ordinary articles 2 pages each, 3 articles two and half pages each and the remaining articles were of 3 pages each.

There was a story which cov-

cred 8 pages. 4 short stories on half page each. Remaining short stories on 3 pages each.

According to the rules of the magazine each advertiser and writer was to receive a copy of the magazine together with a copy of the relevant cutting. This was free of charge.

Now you are required to tell: How many copies of the magazine were sent free of charge to the contributors (including ads)? How many copies of the magazine had to be used for the cuttings?

It may be remembered that even those who had contributed to the cover, i.e. the two photographers, were also to be supplied with a cutting of the cover as well as the magazine.

■■

This is a little choosy, but only a little.

One morning Ramesh bought a *paan* (beetle-leaf) from a *paanwala* and gave him a fifty-paise coin. Since the *paan* was worth 25 paise, Ramesh had to take back 25 paise. The *paanwala* said to him, "Babuji, I do not have 25 paise. But, if you give me a one-rupee note, I shall return 75 paise."

How could that be? Can you guess?

Kundan's father brought a toy for him. This toy was fitted with a wooden strip. There were three thick nails 'A', 'B' and 'C' fitted to the strip. There were 35 plates made of brass on nail 'A'. These square plates were fitted in such a way that each plate was smaller in size than the one placed below it. The remaining nails 'B' and 'C' had no plates.

The plates on nail 'A' were to be removed one by one and placed on nail 'C' in such a way that the bigger plate should be below the smaller plate (as was on nail 'A'). There were some important guidelines and rules to be observed while removing the plates. They are as under:

1. Only one plate to be removed at a time.

2. Nail 'B' can be used while removing the plates.

3. At no time or place the bigger plates were to be placed over the smaller plates.

4. In any case, any of the three nails was to be used for keeping a plate.

Kundan had removed 25 plates and began to play with 10 plates It took him one hour and ten minutes. in playing with the ten plates. As per the rules he removed the plates from nail 'A' to nail 'C'.

Kundan's friend Rajendra studied this toy and asked Kundan if he could remove all the 35 plates

from nail 'A' to nail 'C' and if so, in how much time.

After thinking for a moment, Kundan replied that he could remove the plates within 7 to 8 hours.

Rajendra was not satisfied. He challenged Kundan to do it within the stipulated time. Kundan accepted the challenge. After some time Kundan found out that it was not easy and Rajendra was right.

For this purpose he made a machine which speeded up the interchanging of plates 20 times.

Do you think Kundan will be able to transfer the plates from nail 'A' to 'C', with the help of this machine? What time do you think the machine will take to complete this? ■■

A Burning Problem

98

It all happened on 4 November. It was 8 p.m. There was a hue and cry in Maujpur that Cloth merchant Badri Nath's wife had caught fire. On receiving this information Badri Nath reached home.

By the time his two neighbours Radheshyam and Mangat Lal, hearing Rukmini's shouts reached the place of accident, she had become unconscious. Her nylon saree had caught fire.

The two tried to put out fire by using blankets. This took quite some time.

Two minutes after Badri Nath's arrival Police Inspector Premdas who got information of the accident through some source, arrived with his force.

He inspected the place of accident, found Rukmini lying on the floor of the kitchen, arranged to send her to a city hospital nearby and started minute inspection.

and enquiries.

Observations:

Kitchen light was on. There was an extinguished stove in a corner with a milk pot on it. Gas-cylinder was placed on a shelf in another place. Its regulator was open so was the knob of the burner but no gas smell was emitting from the cylinder.

The inspector could not find any kerosene tin or an extinguished match stick anywhere. He was told, on enquiry, that kerosene stock had finished in the morning itself.

While Premdas began suspecting some foul play, Rukmini's brother arrived and claimed it to be an attempt to murder his sister.

Prem Das obtained a written complaint from Rukmini's brother, Randhir, treated it as 'an attempt-to-murder case' and proceeded with further enquiries.

Randhir had not pin-pointed his doubt on anyone. Rukmini was not in a position to give statement. Naturally, Premdas started questioning the neighbours.

The statements in a nut-shell:

1. Badri Nath loved his wife.
2. They had no child.
3. He used to return home by 10 or 10:30 at night.

This was what the neighbours said.

Badri Nath said, "I have no personal enmity with any body". He could not place his doubt on anybody.

Kamala, her neighbour, had seen Rukmini going out along with Badri Nath at 3:30 that afternoon. Badari Nath returned home alone at 4 p.m. His wife had gone to her parents. Badri Nath was in the house for 10 to 15 minutes before going out again. Rukmini came back at 7 p.m., entered the house and after some time began to shout for help.

Statement of Badri Nath's servant showed that the Lala had come home at 3 p.m. and returned by 4:30 p.m. He did not oftenly came home at noon. He used to close the shop at 8 p.m. and leave for home.

Sagar Mal, the Gas Agency owner said that a new cylinder was supplied on 28 October. Dates of supply of cylinder in the previous months as told by Sagar Mal were: 8 August, 19 June and 18 September.

Badri Nath agreed with this. A statement from Jagat Ram showed that Badari Nath used to visit a house located in the suburb of the city. There lived his lady-love Rajni with whom he used to spend at least 1 or 2 hours everynight.

"I have heard that Badri Nath meets her expenses," said one Pritam Das.

Badri Nath did not contradict the above two statements.

Premdas and his officers studied the statements and one fine morning on 6 November, Badri Nath was arrested. He did not resist.

Why was the Lala arrested for murder charge? Discuss your points in brief.

■■

Seth Dulichand had 7 sons but none seemed interested in his business.

His sons were : Ram Nivas, Roshan Lal, Dharam Das, Seva Nath, Matu Ram, Khushi Ram and Fateh Chand.

When Dulichand was taken ill he was worried about his business: 'Who would look after it?' he thought.

Somehow, during his illness the boys showed eagerness to know the tricks of the trade. Dulichand deputed his sons to take over his 5 shops, 1 mill and 1 studio. Soon each was busy with his own concern.

Dulichand recovered from his illness and after one year assessed their profits individually. They had all done well but there was a snag.

One day he assembled all his sons and told them that although they had all done well Fateh Chand's assets were less than the

others. So, he directed each of them to contribute to him an amount equal to that which Fateh Chand had already got. They did as directed but in this distribution, Khushi Ram fell short. Now each son had to give Khushi Ram an amount equal to what he possessed. At each distribution one son used to be left with less balance so the distribution process continued as stated above.

Wonder of wonders was that at the end of this cycle, each son had equal amount which lay between 10 and 20 lakhs.

Now, here is your problem:

(a) How much each son had earned?

(b) How much balance was left with each one? ■■

Harish was strolling along the Vasco harbour one late evening when he spotted a deep-sea fishing boat in the harbour. Over its side he saw a rope ladder hanging with its end just touching the water. Rungs of the ladder were one foot apart.

Since it was a full-moon night, the tide started rising. The tide rose at the rate of eight inches an hour. Harish stood wondering at the fast rate of the tide and started calculating how many of the rungs will be covered by midnight exactly at the end of six hours?

■■

Famous scientist Setu Sadan had established his laboratory on an isolated island for quite some years now. He had been experimenting to find out a liquid which would dissolve anything and everything.

One day his assistant, Dr Shanti Raman told him jubilantly that he had been successful in finding the formula for making the desired liquid.

Setu Sadan was delighted but suddenly he appeared sad and disappointed. A complex problem about which he was hitherto unaware tickled him and benumbed his brain.

What could be the Doctor's problem? ■■

SOLUTIONS

1. Minimum expenditure Rs. 4,25,920 (If the value of *pi* is taken as 22/7).

    Note : Minimum circumference of the area is feasible only in circular shape.

2.

S.No. of candidate	Constituency	Defeated by votes	Election No. contested
1. Khuda Baksh	Sidhauda	99,998	4
2. Gurubaksh Singh	Dhansai (R)	1,35,971	1
3. Jacob, R.	Peerwada	35	5
4. Param Priya Das	Khichadbas	4,191	2
5. Banwari Prasad	Banku (R)	71,917	3

    Note : 1. Muslims and Christians cannot contest from 'R' constituencey:

    2. Must obtain 1/6 of total votes cast to save security from being confiscated.

3.

Player	Bowler	How out	Runs
Gavaskar	Kasim	Bold	46 or more
Chetan	Saraf Raj	c by. Bari	46
Surendra	Mushtaq	c.by Miandad	36
Kapil Dev	Imran	c. by Haroon	8
Bedi	–	Run out	1

    Note : 1. The score-card does not indicate the name of the fielder who makes a batsman run-out..

    2. On no-ball, a player can be made run-out but cannot be made catch-out.

    3. Caught by wicket-keeper on some bowler's bowling.

4. Total papers in Sethji's Box 6926.

    Note : 1. Figures in blank spaces in serial order : 11,12,15,19, 31, 774,1586 and 38.

    2. Outer columns contain figures from : 1 to 16

    3. Inner columns contain the total of two figures.

    4. Sq. of total of odd numbers-even numbers = 3rd column.

    5. Last column = total of 1st three columns.

5. Assume T12 or T13 contains a 5, then by (m) 11 must contain 5 so by (J) T8 and T10 would contain 5s fall consecutively. So T12 and T13 do not have 5s, therefore, the 5s are in Tricks 8,9,10,11.

    Moreover, all 10s are accounted for and no 5s are available for T1,2,3, so T3 (SL)

= 9, so by (c) and (e) T1,2,3 become:

1.	2	3	4	6
2.	-	6	7	8
3.	8	9	-	-

Now, Tricks 1,2,6,7 contain no picture-cards, neither by (g) does T5 so the remaining eight hands contain all 16 picture cards, so by (6) each contains exactly two of them. Consider the picture cards in T4, T12 and T13.

Taking into account (f) and (1), we can show:

| T4(H) | | T4(SH) | = | T12(H) | T12(SH) = | T13(H) | | T13(SH) |
| A | | K | | K | | Q | Q | | J |

Since two Ks and two Qs are now accounted for the two picture cards of (the identical) Tricks 8,10,11 must be As and Js, leaving two Ks and two Qs to fill the vacancies in 3 and 9.

Since two of every value (except 5) have been assigned, the three identical Tricks 8,10,11 must each have a 5, so by m, T9 must have 5.

By (k) we can show that T9 must have 5 forcing 8 and 9 to complete the top end of Ts. You should now be able to assign the only remaining eight cards (9,6,4,4,3,3,2,2).

Ans :
1st 6,4,3,2;   2nd 8,7,6,4;   3rd K, Q, 9, 8;   4th A, K, 3, 2;
5th 9,8,7,4;   6th 6,4,3,2;   7th 10,9,8,7;   8th A,J,10,5;
9th K, Q,7,5;   10th A, J, 10,5;   11th A,J,10,5;   12th K,Q,3,2;
13th Q, J,9,6.

6.

Film	Hero	Heroine	Director	Musician
Asha	Rakesh	Rama	Chopra	Soni-Toni
Parvana	Prem	Lata	Rai	Khan Sahib
Sansar	Veerendra	Radha	Tandon	Jwala Bhai
Hamare Liye	Satish	Yogita	Sen	Moni-Rai

7. Amit Kumar will travel from house to office by Circular service No. 2, halting at alternate station. Train halts at 5 stations, and at the rate of 14 paise per stop, he will pay only 70 paise.

8. Total participants 3576. 'A' country-324, 'B'-30 and 'C'-570.

Note : Sq. root of 324900 is 570. 'B' country participants are from 10 to 31. There are two figures of 3 digits and shifting their place gives a 6-digit figure which is a complete square.

9. The gentleman was Lajwanti Devi's father-in-law from aunt's side. (Aunt's husband)

Note: He could even be her father-in-law. But since Sarita was her neighbour she should have known Lajwanti's father-in-law, they all being from a village where people know each other more closely than in a city.

10.

Player	Runs	Bowler	How was he out
1. Javed Miandad	151	M. Amarnath	c.by Gavaskar
2. Qadir	61	Dilip Doshi	c. by D. Doshi
3. Zahir	0	Kapil	c. by Madan Lal
4. Imran Khan	8	Madan Lal	c. by M.Amarnath
5. Mohsin Khan	92	Dilip Doshi	st. by Kirmani.

• Captain : Imran Khan

11.
1. Gordon Greenidge, b. Shastry ....33 runs.
2. Larry Gomes, lbw Venkat Raghvan ....42 runs.
3. Desmond Hynes, c. Gavaskar, b. Shastry ....5 runs.
4. V.Richards, c. Kirmani b. Sandhu ....20 runs.
5. G. Logie, c. Gavaskar, b. Shastry ....4 runs.
6. Clive Lloyd, St. Kirmani, b. Kapil ....76 runs.
7. J. Dujon, c. Vengsarkar, b. Maninder ....89 runs.
8. Joel Garner n.o. ....30 runs.
9. Malcom Marshal, c. Shastry, b. Kapil ....15 runs.
10. Andy Roberts, run out ....4 runs.
11. Michaiel Holding, c. Sandhu, b. Mohinder ....0 zero.
Extras ....27 runs
Total runs 357

12. The position of players in Ento Olympics was as under:

Players	Country	Sport	Position
Kimrochneva	America	Gymnastic	8th
Che Wang	Korea	Diving	7th
Fu Chin	China	Race	5th
Bejobachanev	Romania	Javelin throw	6th
Masakirie	Japan	Swimming	4th

13. Satyender, Baljeet and Seth Jagdish Lal—Present Age 23, 21 and 49, respectively. Car No. 1961.

14. Chint Raman's survey was not genuine.
Note : Chint Raman:

Houses claimed as surveyed by him	=	414
Actual	=	304
'Jaire' in all houses	=	140
'Tejari' in all houses	=	132
'Priya' in all houses	=	126
Total bicycles	=	396

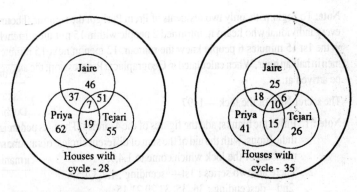

2. Lakhan Chand

Houses surveyed as per his report	=	176
Actual	=	176
'Jaire' in all houses	=	59
'Tejari' in all houses	=	57
'Priya' in all houses	=	84
Total bicycles	=	200

15. The engine will push wagon 'A' up to point 'D'; will return to crossing 'J' and proceed towards new station; push wagon 'B' to 'D' and connect 'A' with 'B' and will arrive at the old station via Parvat Nagar New Station. At crossing 'J', 'A' will be pushed to Jeevan Nagar and 'B' towards Parvat Nagar New Station. It will then pull 'A' and push 'B' from behind 'A' and go to point 'D', leave 'B' there, take 'A' back to new station and going via old station, 'B' will be taken to old station. The engine will then return to Jeevan Nagar.

16. Seven and a half miles.

   Note 1. When I asked the first question, we must have done 1/3rd of the journey.

   2. At second question 2/5th.

   3. $2/5 - 1/3 = 1/15$ which was to be half a mile.

   4. The whole journey (15/15th) must then have been 7 and a half miles.

17. A = 6, B =56, C= 576

   Note: The puzzle has three series. The third series is the product of second and first series.

18. Total passengers boarded at Delhi = 197.

   Total passengers availing first ever flight in 'Samrat' – 493.

   Note: Passengers going to Scotland were in odd numbers. They were equal to the cube root of 1/10 of the passengers that landed in England. Under these circumstances 3 is the only figure, the cube root of which is 27 and passengers getting down at London were – 270.

19. Total population of Prem Puri 3,55,527.

Note: To begin with, only two residents of Prem Puri got the rumour. Thereafter, every individual who heard it, informed 2 people within 15 minutes. In this way in the 1st 15 minutes 6 people knew the rumour. 12 men in next 15 minutes. 18 men in half an hour. When calculated in Geographical Progression, the answer can be arrived at.

20. The secret Nos. of the lock —1497

    Note : 1. Fill in the blanks; add the figures of the 4 circles. Then, as per the given indications, with the aid of the sum of different circles, obtain the secret numbers of the lock which come to 1,4,9,7

          2. There are two series : 1st—ascending : 1,2,3,4,5,6
             2nd—descending : 36, 35, 33,29,21,15
             By multiplying figures of small columns, figures from inner circles are obtained.

          3. 1028 is added to all figures of both outer circles, and sum of figures from smallest circles is deducted from it.

21. (a) Virbhadra reached Luxury Palace by shorter route.
    (b) Distance from Arampur to Luxury Palace was 160 miles by longer route.
    Note : 1. Virbhadra – rested for 48 minutes. He was riding for 4 hours and 12 minutes.
           Ramendra - rested for 36 minutes, riding for 6 hours 24 minutes.
          2. Ramendra travelled seven times the rest taken by Virbhadra it means that he rode 8 times more than the period taken by Virbhadra for resting.

22.

Name of the club	Place	Boy	Girl
Dhairyashali	Tilak Nagar	Ramesh Nagarath	Geeta Singh
Imagination	Ramakrishnapuram	Kailash Thakur	Sulabha Karkare
Vikassheel	Karol Bagh	Jacob Smith	Asha Ghosh
Aap Aur Hum	Rohtas Nagar	Satwant Singh	Mrinalini
Kalpnasheel	Sarojini Nagar	Imran Khan	Rama Arora

23. There are 4 Arithmetical Series in this problem as under :
    (1) 3, 4, 5, 6, 7, 8, 9, 10, 11, ...
    (2) 6, 5, 8, 7, 10, 9, 12, 11, 14 ......
    (3) 18, 20, 40, 42, 70, 72, 108, 110, 154, ...
    (4) 3, 11, 17, 29, 39, 55, 69, 89, 107 ......
    Thus, the blanks are – 70, 39, 9, 12, 108, 69, 10, 11, 110, 89, 11, respectively.

24. The total age of all 5 = 221 years.
    Note : 1. Sharbati Devi—91 years, Shanti Devi—73 years, Saraswati Devi—37 years, Savita —19 years and Ranjan—1 year.
          2. Last digits of ages during last year are formed from 0, 2, 4, 6, 8. This year their age is one of the following figures 1, 3, 5, 7, 9. As there is figure 5, there is figure 4 for last year.

25. Total seats —1005, Lower stall—180, Middle stall —220 Upper stall —320, Balcony—285.

Note: Four shows in a day. 5 paise per ticket!
1. Total seats 1005.
2. Lower stall possible vacant seats-111, 222, 333, 444.
3. Lower stall vacant seats are less than all stall vacant seats together. Therefore, lower stand vacant seats can be 111. If 222 or more, income from 'Kaner Ke Phul', cannot be assessed correctly.

26. Girl's name —Durga Devi. The name of the boy — Dudh Nath.

Note : It would be seen that all names are given serial-wise on the basis of the use of vowels.

27. Suresh gets there first and Ramesh misses the train. Ramesh tries to arrive a short time before 4:05 by his watch, but 4:05 by his watch is actually 4:15 correct time. Suresh tries to arrive a short time before 3:50 by his watch which means correct time is 3:45.

28. Water level will be reduced. While the bowl containing balls was floating, it had raised water level in proportion to its weight and size. After it immersed in water, it displaced water according to its volume. Water affected by weight is more than the water displaced by volume (otherwise the bowl and balls would not have sunk). Therefore, water level is reduced.

29. Numbers 12, 21, 26, 41 is the only combination totalling 100.

30. A —64, B— 9, C— 66, D—324, E—463

Note : 1 . The figure of this circle is the square of the sum of external figure.

2 . This figure is obtained by adding the figure in the smaller circle to the figure in the outer portion of the larger circle and then subtracting the figure in the inner portion of the bigger circle from it.

3. The square of the difference of figures at note 2 above are here.

4. The sum of the outer figures in the bigger circles are in the semi-circle.

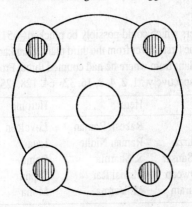

31. Car No. DIB 3672
    Note: 1. Since the first figure is one and a half times the last figure, the possible figures can be 3, 6, 9 (for first place) and 2,4,6 (for the last place).
    2. Since the figures in first two digits are half of those in the last two digits, they cannot be 6, 9 and 4, 6.
    3. Possibly at second place they are 1 or 6, and at the third place 6 or 7.

32. Height of Gagan Chumbi —113.93 ft.
    Lower - end of the ladder
    and resting point at wall-distance— 52.63 ft.
    Note : $(A + 36)^2 + (B + 36)^2 = (125.5)^2$ ...(1)
    $$A/36 = 36/B$$
    $$A B = 36^2 = 1296 ... (2)$$
    (See figure below)

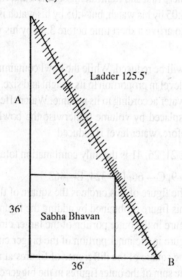

Ladder 125.5'

A

36' Sabha Bhavan

36' B

33. Maximum flowers which could possibly be plucked —511
    After plucking the first flower from the third plant, Shankar would pluck flowers from the same plant from where he had counted three. From maximum 9 plants he can pluck, respectively : 1, 2, 4, 8, 16, 32, 64, 128, 256.

34.

S. No.	Films	Hero	Heroine	Director
1.	Arpana	Rakesh Ranjan	Loveleen	Prem Tilak
2.	Chalta Purza	Raman Nidhe	Lata	Pramod Goswami
3.	Swapna Sansar	S. Sharma	Rama	Ratan Jeet
4.	Karma Dweep	Mrinal Rai	Sapna	S. Burman
5.	Seva Ashram	M. Verma	Mona	Arif Khan

138

35.

Team	India	Spain	Holland	Aus.	Russia	Mal.	Kenya	Total Points
India	–	equal	equal	won	won	won	won	10
Spain	equal	–	equal	won	won	won	won	10
Holland	equal	equal	–	won	equal	equal	won	8
Australia	lost	lost	lost	–	won	won	won	6
Russia	lost	lost	equal	lost	–	won	lost	3
Malaysia	lost	lost	equal	lost	lost	–	won	3
Kenya	lost	lost	lost	lost	won	lost	–	2

36.

S.No.	Name of husband	Name of wife	Savings of the couple
(1)	Jagat Narayan	Devi	Rs. 6,825
(2)	Banarasi Das	Lakshmi	Rs. 1,900
(3)	Motilal	Sushila	Rs. 7,875
(4)	Sita Ram	Rukmani	Rs. 8,400

Note: Total savings are Rs. 25000/-. The couple saving maximum is Sita Ram and Rukmini.

Hint:

Husband/wife	Rukmani 2,100	Lakshmi 1,500	Sushila 3,500	Devi 2,275
Sita Ram (Wife x 3)	6,300	4,500	10,500	6,825
Banarasi Das (Wife x 1/4)) + 25	550	400	900	593.25
Moti Lal (Wife x 1.25)	2,625	1,875	4,375	2843.25
Jagat Narayan (Wife x 2)	4,200	3,000	7,000	4,550

37. Prakash was the ring leader

Member	Driver	Car No.	Destination
Abhishek	Durga Prasad	DLZ -1980	Srinagar
Ashok	Govind	DLZ-2222	Shimla
Nishikant	Meva Lal	DLZ-3443	Nainital
Prakash	Sohan Lal	DLZ-1001	Dehra Dun
Bhanu Pratap	Maha Singh	DLZ-2134	Kulu

38. Master Vasant Raj has been teaching for 37 years. He is 60, Mahabir 32 and Arvind 12 years old.

39. Ramesh Mohan succeeded his father.
    Profit of each son was as under:
    1. Ram Mohan —Rs. 100
    2. Shyam Mohan—Rs. 600
    3. Tejender Mohan —Rs. 600

    4. Ramesh Mohan —Rs. 2000
    5. Pankaj Mohan —Rs. 2000
    6. Chandra Mohan—Rs. 300

Note :

Son (Name/Profit & factor) Sr. N. of Son	2nd son 200	3rd son 300	4th son 400	5th son 500
Sham Mohan (2 Times)	400	600	800	1000
Tejander Mohan (3 Times)	600	900	1200	1500
Ramesh Mohan (4 Times)	800	1200	1600	2000
Pankaj Mohan (5 times)	1000	1500	2000	2500

2. Profit, youngest & eldest sons — Rs. 100 + 300 = Rs. 400
   Profit remaining sons = Rs. 5200
   As per the table, maximum profit —Rs. 5400
   Minimum profit —Rs. 4400

40. Water Tank, behind Rashtri Adarsh Vidyalaya, of 'Capital's
    Water Supply Corporation' – Capacity 2,40,19,801 Ltrs.

    Note : The figure arrived at is obtainable by shifting places of two complete
    squares of the four-digit figure which comes to eight-digit complete
    square.

41. 2,00,000 (two lacs) litres.

    Note : 1. Capacity of tank was from 10 lacs to 90 lacs litres.
           2. Formula to find out x (capacity of pipe) :–
              Total drainage 7 1/2 hrs. $\therefore$ $1/15 + 1/x + 1/2x + 1/2 x = 2/15$ x = 30
              $\therefore$ Capacity of Palace water supply was 30th part of the tank.

42. The pier and the lighthouse are on opposite sides of the hotel.

43.

Generator producing country	Hours in use	Electricity Produced
Germany	6 hrs.	1800 units
England	4 hrs.	1600 units
Russia	9 hrs.	5400 units
Japan	7 hrs.	4900 units

Notes :

Generator/Unit	hours	4	6	7	9
Germany	300	1200	1800	2100	2700
England	400	1600	2400	2800	3600
Russia	600	2400	3600	4200	5400
Japan	700	2800	4200	4900	6300

These generators can produce:

Maximum – (1200 + 2400+ 4200 + 6300) = 14100 units.

Minimum – (2700 + 2800 + 3600 + 2800) = 11900 units.

44. Ram Nathji's servant was Dilip.

Guess in Short:

Seva Dasji did not hear Ranjit. So, if Ranjit is Danga Nath's man, he would lie that he is Ram Nath's man. And if he is really the servant of Ram Nath, then he would say so.

Seva Das did hear what Dilip said. He had repeated what Ranjit had said. He spoke the truth and he was Ram Nath's man.

If we consider Ranjit or Panthe as Ram Nath's men, then all statements made by everyone would be contradictory to each other.

If we take Ranjit as Ram Nath's servant it would mean that his statement that the other two are Danga Nath's servant would be true. That would mean that the remaining two lied whereas Dilip had repeated what Ranjit had whispered. This proves that Ranjit had lied.

Suppose we take Panthe's statement as correct (that he is Ram Nath's servant), then his statement that Dilip is Danga Nath's man proves incorrect and hence false.

45.

Smuggler	Mode of Transport/Article smuggled	Destination
Victor	On Foot/ Morphine	Madras
Ajay	Bullock Cart/ L.S.D.	Delhi
Jeevan Das	Bus/Heroin	Calcutta
Robert	Car/Gold Biscuits	Agra
Inder	Truck/ Diamond	Bombay
	Gang leader —Rajiv	

46. The lead equation $x = 5y = 26$ tells you that cannot be less than 6 (otherwise you couldn't subtract 26 from 5y). The suggested second equation will yield $Z = 52 - 8y$, which means that y cannot be more than 6. If it can be neither more than nor less than 6, it must be 6. From our first equation above this makes $x = 4$, and from the second, $z = 4$. The rest is easy.

141

Ans. (Pile 1) 12 Blacks and 4 Reds.
(Pile 2) 6 Blacks and 18 Reds.
(Pile 3) 8 Blacks and 4 Reds.

47. Ranjit Babu would travel by ordinary bus along with his family.

48. Length of the rope 38—feet.
Note : Laxman's field was circular.

49. The question was asked by Alka to Radha on 29.2.1980.
Note: Radha was 12 years of age on 29.2.76. On her next birthday (on 29.2 84),
she will be 20 years old. She would be studying for her M.A., then.

50.

Candidate	Position	Proposer	Supporter	Votes secured
Ashish Banerji	Chairman	Mayadin	Satish, Kumar Sethi	405
Bhim Bali Verma	Chief Secy.	R. Goyal	Mayadin	369
Shivchandra Saxena	Management Secretary	Bhola Nath	P. Gupta	351
Dr. Bhaskar Rai	Org. Secy.	Ganga Pd.	Darshan Lal	270

51. This is how both the trains will be manoeuvred:
(1) The engine of the empty wagons will carry 20 wagons and stay on the second
rail line. The remaining 20 empty wagons will stay where they were. These
will be joined to the front of the engine with loaded wagons to be taken ahead.
In the meantime the engine stationed on second rail lines will carry 20 wagons
toward Dumbrali. It will then stop at a little distance.
(2) The engine of the loaded wagons will now carry 20 empty wagons, will return
and leave empty wagons on any rail line. It will go back a little and proceed
towards Domrer through an unoccupied line.
(3) The engine of the empty wagons will go back with 20 wagons, pick up the 20
wagons stationed on the line and proceed towards its destination.

52. The average speed of Randhir's scooter – 26.4 km / hr.
The scooter covered total distance – 22.22 km.
Note : Half circumference of inner circle : 3.5 metre.
Half circumference of outer circle – 3.535 metre.
Length outer end – 22.22 metre.

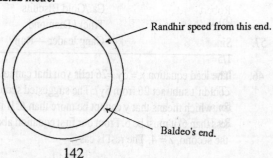

Randhir speed from this end.

Baldeo's end.

53. Mange Lal wanted to withdraw Rs. 38.99 from the bank but by mistake he withdrew Rs.99.38.

Note: 1. Since he withdrew rupees in place of paise and vice-versa, both the amounts (i.e. Rs. & Paise) cannot exceed figure 99.

2. Suppose the withdrawn amount is Rs. A and Paise B, then, 100A+B– 2140 = 2 x (100 B +A). In other words;

98A – 199 B = 2140 – (1)

.3. In order to arrive at the second equation we have to take into account 40 paise that he had spent.

This gives the following equation:

B – 40=2A or 2A = B – 40

100 + B – 40 = 2 A or 2A = B + 60.

200 + B – 40 = 2 A or 2A = B + 160.

Now, out of the above three equations only one would agree with the first obtained equation 98A–199B = 2140, which determines the value of 'A' & 'B'.

54.

S.No.	Name	Order of merit	Name of ship	Rank
1.	Daljeet	Second	Delhi	V. Admiral
2.	Sudarshan	Fifth	Mysore	Captain
3.	Jacob	First	Kashmir	Commodore
4.	Balbir	Third	Dhavalgiri	Commander
5.	Safdar	Fourth	Nilgiri	R. Admiral

55. Lattooji was married in 1947. An error is likely to occur when Randhir· is considered 3 years of age on his third birthday. He was only 2 at that time.

56. Sant Kumar kept awaking for maximum 1 hr. 15 mts. and minimum 15 minutes, in order to know the time.

At the time when Sant Kumar kept awaking for maximum time, bullet was fired at 1:14 or 12:29 a.m.

The time of firing depends on:

(a) If the bird coos 7th time only once (7 includes first two coos), then the shot was fired at 12:14 a.m.

(b) If 7th time she coos twice then the shot was fired at 12:29 a.m.

57. Since T started with 1/5 of the total pool and finishing with 1/4, he won 1/4 – 1/5=1/20. Similarly J won 1/3–1/4 =1/12, so together they won, 2/15. So B must have Lost 2/15 which, we are told, was Rs. 2. Therefore, the pool was Rs. 15/- . T's finishing total was 1/4 of this, J's 1/3, and B's the remainder. Hence, Tahir finished with Rs. 3.75, Jamal with Rs. 5/-, Billu with Rs. 6.25. (having started with Rs 3/-, Rs. 3.75, Rs 8.25 respectively).

143

58. Total houses in Padampur – 889.
Tubes in 62 houses, bulbs in 761 houses,
23 houses petromax and 223 houses had lamps.

59. Ram Nath's last year's capital – Rs. 57,69,604/-.

60. What Balram was talking about had taken place 16 years ago. On the day of their conversation, Balram was 64 years old and Ravindra was 32 years old.

61. $86292 \div 12 = 7191$.

Note : 1. As per the formula (B–A) =1, $\therefore$ B = A + 1.
2. The diviser is in two digits. When we multiply it with 7, the product should also be in two digits. For this, the diviser will be one of the following: 10,11,12,13 & 14. Now, in the third step, the product is in three digits which could be obtained only by 12, 13 and 14.
3. But with 14, the figures in the third step cannot be arrived at in 3 digits.
4. With 12, it will be A=1 and B = 2. This will obtain : 12 x 7191 = 86292 wherein A and B will be equal.
5. With 13, it will be A =5 and B = 6.
Now it will be : 13 x 7585 = 92605, A =5, B =6. And, 13 x 7595 = 92735 A = 5 B = 7.

62. Balbir Singh is not entitled to any priority in any category of the Housing Schemes. He had received an award from Lord Cornwallis who was Governor - General of India during 1786 to 1793. And, there could hardly be any possibility that the Subedar Sahib was alive.

63. Seth Jamna Das was to receive from the following persons the amounts as shown against each.

(1) Dineshwale – Rs. 21,90,621.10
(2) Rameshji – Rs. 12,02,351.10
(3) Shambhu Nath – Rs. 48,01,241.10
(4) Banwari Lal – Rs. 16,97,561.10
Total —Rs. 98,91,774.40

Note : 1. A,B,E,C,J,Z, T, X,Y, L stand for separate digits.
2. 4A = J, comes twice which indicates that no digit is carried forward. 4 x =x also indicates no carried forward. When it comes to $4x = x$, x = 0 4A = J, It will be : A =1,2 and J = 4,8
3. In top to bottom first line L+A+J+A+ carried forward (if any) = Z proves that J is not equal to 8. This gives us A =1, J = 4.
4. If in the third line it is : 2Z + 2 x + 1 (carried forward) = Z + carried forward (if any), thus it gives 2Z +1 = Z + 10 (carried forward) Z = 9.
5. From Z = 9 in the first line, L + 1+4+1 + carried forward (1 or 2) = 9 will arrive at L = 2 (because A is equal to 1).
6. 1 +2 +Y + T + 1 (carried forward) = Y + 10 (carried forward) 4 + Y + T = Y + 10 $\therefore$ T = 6.
7. Sixth line : $\therefore$ 2 + B +4+6 = E + 10 or

144

$B = E+10 - 12x = E - 2$ or $E - B = 2$

$\therefore$ $E = 7$ or $B = 5$ or 3.

But in the 5th line it is $1+6+C+2+B=E+10$

Which gives $C + B = E + 1$

$C = E - B + 1 = 3$ makes $B = 5$, $E = 7$

$Y = 8$.

64. The wife of poet Veerdev said that king Chatursen had never given him even an inch let alone a triangular piece of land, as the length of any two sides of a triangle was not more than the length of the third side. The total of two sides of the 'triangular piece of land' awarded to him by king Chatursen ($150^2/_3$ yards and 45 yards 3 inches) was equal to the third side ($195^3/_4$ yards). So the awarded land was nothing but a simple line.

65. Captain Premswaroop is Shalini's murderer.

Reasoning : If we take Bishna as the killer, two sentences, first and the third, of his statement prove to be false. It is to be noted that each suspected criminal has given only one false statement. This puts to an end the possibility of Bishna being the killer.

Similarly, if we take D'Souza as the killer, two of his sentences, first and third, prove to be false. So, he is not the killer. As regards Karim, if we take him for a killer, his first sentence becomes false. We cannot decide whether or not his second and third sentences are correct. But if we take Karim as the killer, Captain Premswaroop's third sentence proves to be incorrect. Under these circumstances, the Captain's remaining two sentences should be considered to be correct. His second sentence establishes his friendship with Karim. Which in turn proves incorrect Karim's third sentence, "I do not know Captain Prem Swaroop". This makes two of his sentences incorrect and proves that he is not the killer.

When we consider the Captain as the killer we see that each criminal has given only one incorrect statement. This proves the point that the Captain is the killer of Shalini.

66. Fauja Singh is 65 years old, Jarnail Singh is 41 and Shamsher Singh is 17 years old.

Note : There can be many possibilities in solving this equation. But, the reference to Hitler establishes the fact that Fauja Singh lived and fought during the Second World War. He received the medal in 1945, which is the base of the above calculation.

67. Number of words in Professor Sham Nath's Dictionary, 'Bhaskar-Kosh' are – 10,26,425. Number of pages in 'Diwakar–Kosh' are – 1970.

Note: In all circumstances the words in 'Diwakar–Kosh' would be between 9,37,377 and 9,99,999. When we add 522 to these the minimum number of words amount to 9,37,899. This means the number of pages fall between 969 to 1000. As per the conditions, the figures arrive at 9,63,802 and the square root of this figure works out to be 982.

68. The speed of the car – 90 km per hour. Distance between Air Port and Surajmal's factory - 270 km.

Distance covered by bullock-cart – 16.67 km.

(This is the distance which Surajmal covered by bullock-cart before getting into the car).

Note: Surajmal reached 15 minutes earlier than usual time. He had taken 5 minutes in transhipment. This means he saved 10 minutes' time compared to usual time taken by him in earlier trips between Air Port and his factory.

69. Length of Jamnagar Mail – 800 feet. Average speed – 70 mph or 115 km. Length of Ahmedabad Express – 960 feet.

Average speed – 50 mph. (or 80 km.)

Note: Both trains are less than 1000 feet in length. The total length of both trains is more than 1,550 feet and less than 1,840 feet.

70.

Award	State	Producer	Programme
First	Gujarat	M.D' Souza	Bungalow of flowers
Second	Kerala	Gafoor Khan	A tea estate
Third	Haryana	Raghuveer Singh	Village life
Special	Punjab	K.L. Gupta	Harvest
Consolation	Assam	Prem Da	The army on the front

71. The way to 25 plants to be planted in 22 rows is shown below in three different figures (5 plants in each row):

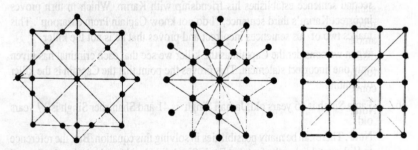

72. Shyam Chandra can measure from 1 inch to 36 inches of cloth by marking the plate at 4 minimum places. There are two ways to mark the plates as shown in the figures below:

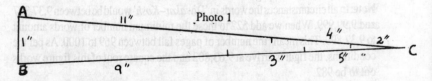

146

Photo 2

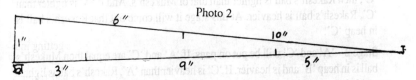

73. Sethji carried the show-piece by placing it horizontally. The restriction of 2 feet are for the height and not for the length of any article.

74. The total of figures of all 18 circles —2877.

   Note : 1. Figures in blank columns : 11, 165, 191, 307, 411.
   2. 1st column figures : 10 to 15 in ascending order.
   3. Inner columns – square of first columns – the figures of that column.
   4. To the total of figures in innermost circle and central column 1 has been added to and taken from alternately.

75. The total number of birds had become – 93,312, in each island, after the King's orders. Total birds in all islands–5,59,872. Prior to the order of shifting the birds their number, islandwise, was as under:

   (1) Kamaij – 33,614   (2) Samahab – 62,426
   (3) Sadobarba – 87,122   (4) Dad – 1,08,290
   (5) Gobaito– 1,26,434   (6) Nagua – 1,41,986

76. Laxmimal began to doubt when he saw the erroneous spelling of 'eighty five'. He had checked the cheque prior to issuing the token. He had carefully seen the slanting lines and date recorded on the cheque, second observation of the cheque revealed that there was little distance between the figures 8 and 5. The 8 in the amount and the 8 in the date 18.8.87 were quite differently written. There was distinct difference in the handwriting between the amount in figures which were forged and the signature on the cheque. He suspected that five thousand were converted to eightyfive thousand.

   Note: 1. To cross the cheque two slanting lines are marked in the left top corner of the cheque.
   2. The amount of the cheque can be drawn within 6 months of the date of the issue of the cheque.

77. To begin with, we shall divide the 9 balls in 3 heaps of 3 balls each. Suppose the heaps are 'A', 'B' & 'C'

   First weighing
   We will place heap 'A' on one pan of the balance and heap 'B' on the other. There are three possibilities:

   (1) 'A' = 'B' (2) 'A' heavier than 'B' and (3) 'B' heavier than 'A'

   Second weighing :
   Stage 1– Second weighing – 'A' and 'C' to be put on pans. If 'A' is heavier than

147

'C', then Rakesh's ball is lighter than that of Mukesh's. And if 'A' is lighter than 'C', Rakesh's ball is heavier. At this stage it will come out that Rakesh's ball is in heap 'C'.

Stage 2 – 'A' and 'C' will be put on pans. If 'A' and 'C' are equal then Mukesh's ball is in heap 'B' and is heavier. If 'C' is heavier than 'A', Rakesh's ball is lighter and is in heap 'A'.

Stage 3 – 'B' and 'C' will be put on pans. If 'B' and 'C' are equal then Rakesh's ball is heavy and is in heap 'A'. If 'C' is heavier than 'B', then, Rakesh's ball is light and is in 'B' heap. Thus, we would come to know the exact heap where Rakesh's ball exists and whether it is heavy or light in weight in comparison with Mukesh's ball.

Third weighing :
In the third weighing experiment, we take any two balls from Rakesh's heap. Now, if these two weigh equal, the third ball belongs to Rakesh. If the scale is uneven, the raised pan has Rakesh's ball because it (the ball) is lighter and its pan will lift up. In case the ball is heavy, it is in the lower pan of the balance. Weighing these balls three times we find out Rakesh's ball and also know whether it is lighter or heavier than Mukesh's.

78.

Position	Sajjan Singh			Durjan Singh		
	Inf.	Cavalry	Total	Inf.	Cavalry	Total
Before war	76	26	102	318	35	353
Killed in war	20	2	22	232	18	250
After war	56	24	80	86	17	103

Hint : 'A' = 121 (Square of total of both numbers)
'B' = 15 (Total of all numbers)
'C' =33 (Total of B + 18)
'D' = 26 (Total of B + 11).
'E' = 5 (Total of both digits of 32).

Troops of Sajjan Singh:
Infantry : - 11+15+18+20+12 =76
Cavalry :- 8+6+2+5+5 = 26.

Troops of Durjan Singh :
Infantry : 16+12+64+49+25+23+26+33+38+32 = 318.
Cavalry : (1+3) + (5+6) +(4+4) + (3+4) + (2+3) = 35

79. The names of last seven students on the list are:
18. Khairati Lal, 19. Chandgi Ram, 20. Thandi Ram,
21. Narayan Das, 22. Sharad Chand, 23. Zhanda Ram,
24. Banarasi Das.

Note : 1. All names on the list are in special serial order.

2. In this, the next number is with a particular difference from the previous. Series are : 9, 12, 17, 24, 33, 44, 57, 72, 89, 108
Difference: (3) (5) (7) (9) (11) (13) (15) (17) (19).

80. Hawrah Express.

81. Car number – 7980

82. Rajesh Sharad's old Phone No. 589604, new Phone No. 5729604.

83.

Name	Rank	Name of the plane	Time of flight
Balwant Singh	Wg. Comdr.	MIG -21 (fighter)	8.00
E. D, Souza	Sq. Ldr.	Canbera (bomber)	8.10
Ahmad Khan	Flg. Officer	Hunter (fighter)	8.02
Raghuveer P. Singh	Flg. Officer	Gnat (fighter)	8.01
Shrikant	Pilot Officer	Ajit (fighter)	8.03
S. Subramaniam	Pilot Officer	Chetak (H. Copter)	8.20

84. Scooter number of Abhinav – 196;
Saurabh's Motor Cycle No.961;
Their father's Car No. 1157.
Note: 1. Square of numbers from 10 to 31 is in three digits.

2. Only numbers 100, 144, 196, 400 and 900 are such that if their first digits are written at the end, they make a complete square.

85. Only 6 weights of 1,3,9,27,81 and 243 kg.

86. First bullet was fired at 10.26.
Note : 1. The criminals entered the house at 10.24. When the decimal point is removed from it we get 1024 which is a complete square.

2. When we add 8 and deduct 15 from the time reflected in the mirror we get complete square figures. Therefore this time is between two figures of complete squares. That means 2 complete squares of three digits have 23 as the difference. These figures are square of 11 and 12. (That is how the difference of two squares can be 11+12 =23).

3. Figure 136 meets the condition of 8 & 15. The mirror shows 1.36 (Time). Which means actual time to be 10.24. (When we deduct the time seen in the mirror from 12.00, we get the actual time).

87.

Section	Gate	Position before war	Position after war
1.	Ajmeri Gate	1296	3125
2.	Lahori Gate	4026	3125
3.	Delhi Gate	2376	3125
4.	Fatehpur Gate	4651	3125
5.	Jaipur Gate	3276	3125
	Total	15625	15625

Note : 1. Let us suppose the number of soldiers at the gate of each section was respectively A,B,C,D, and E.

2. After the first stage the number of soldiers was : 5A, B–A, D–A, E–A.

3. After second stage the position was :
6A – B, 5 (B–A), C– B, D–B, E–B.

4. In this way the position after the 5th stage was:
6A–5E, 6B–5A–E, 6C–5B–E, 6D–5C–E, 5E–5D.

88.

S.No.	Names of the people	S.H.O.	Thief	Phone No. of S.H.O.
1.	Jacabson	Iqbal Jafar	Nathu	262504
2.	Pradyuman Kumar	Seva Ram	Vicky	615973
3.	Pritam Singh	Nafe Singh	Tenty	371951
4.	Shish Ram	Bhagwan Das	Singhada	43251
5.	Suresh Chandra	Ram Singh	Dinteer	311211

Note : 1. 43251 was not Iqbal Jafar's phone number.

2. Phone number of S.H.O. who arrested Vicky was 615973.

3. No. 371951, the only phone number with odd numbers, was used by Pritam – Pradyuman.

4. Ram Singh's phone number is not 615973.

89. Lock number is – 1902.

Note : 1. Figures in blank columns are : 205, 286, 131, 122, 507 & 651.

2. A careful study reveals that there are, under mentioned, three series:
First : 1_4 5_6 11_8 19_{10} 29_{12} 41_{14} 55_{16} 71_{18} 89_{20} 109_{22} 131.........

Second : 1_1 2_4 6_9 15_{16} 31_{25} 56_{36} 92_{49} 141_{64} 205_{81} 286_{100} 386_{121} 507_{144} 651.

Third : 2_3 5_5 10_7 17_9 26_{11} 37_{13} 50_{15} 65_{17} 82_{19} 101_{21} 122_{23} 145_{25} 170.

90. There will be minimum 6 marks on the white portion of the egg-shaped plate. This will enable Tailor Master Sham Chandra to measure, at one stretch, cloth, from 1 inch to 36 inches. These markings can be done in many ways. The figure below shows three ways:

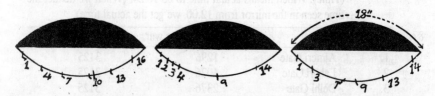

91. According to the plan given by Ashok Rai, Ranchod Das took the Engine from tunnel E and stationed it near wagon 'B'.

The wagon was pulled and the engine came at crossing 'D'.

From there wagon 'B' was pushed and brought to crossing 'C' and placed on the 40 feet railway line piece. The engine now reached crossing 'D' & 'R' (R is shown in the figure) and came up to wagon 'A'. It pushed wagon 'A' and came to crossing 'C', took wagon 'B' and started for Preet Nagar.

Reaching crossing 'R' the engine drove wagon 'B' towards Preet Nagar –Prem Nagar line and left it near the crossing. Wagon 'A' was left on Preet Nagar –Viran Nagar line. Then the engine carried wagon 'B' and pushing wagon 'A' came to crossing 'C', left wagon 'A' there and while returning left 'B' where 'A' was and reached crossing 'D' via 'R' and 'D'. From there pulling wagon 'A' came to 'B' via crossing 'D', left 'A' there and stopped in the tunnel.

92. Ramu's drum was emptied before Khaldu's.

   Note : Liquid flow-out (qty. coming out) depends on the area of the hole it is passing out through. 6 cm. half circular hole-area is:

   $\pi \times 6^2$ that is 36 π sq.cm.

   Circumference of three 5 cm holes is equal to:

   π, 5 2 x 5 2 x 3 = 75.4, which is definitely smaller than the area created by hole made by Ramu.

93. The circle can be divided in:
   Minimum 8 and maximum 29 parts.

   Note : For minimum formula = No. of lines + 1.

   For maximum formula = Total of all lines (from 1 to last number) + 1.

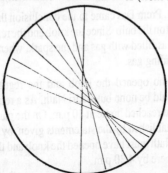

94. There are two parts in this problem. In the first, the speed of the car is to be determined. In the second, the distance between the truck and the car before the truck crossed the bridge is to be worked out. There are two situations on which the answer to part first depends: (i) the car already had reached the 8th pole, (ii) it might be ten feet ahead of 10th pole or 15 feet behind 11th pole.

In the first position the speed of the car would be 1.46 times the speed of the truck. In the second, it would be 1.3 times the speed of the truck.

In either case the car was 750 metres ahead of the truck when the latter reached the other end of the bridge.

95. 132 copies of 'Gyan Patrika' would be needed—including those used for sending cuttings. The details are as follows: – Advertisements and advertisers —89; Writers —12; Poets —17; Short story-writers —7; Novelists —1; Illustrator—1; Photographers —2. Thus 129 copies were required plus three for cuttings, which makes it 132.

96. The *Panwallah* must be having 3 paise coins. And he could pay thus: 25 coins of 3 paise each or 3 coins of 20 paise each and 5 coins of 3 paise each.

97. Kundan would not be able to transfer the plates with the help of the machine. It is almost impossible. If the machine is kept on working for all 24 hours, the 35 plates may take nearly 81635.6 days within the stipulated conditions and rules.

    Note: To transfer one plate, one move is involved, for 2 discs, three moves; for 3, seven moves; for 4, 15 moves are involved. And thus 35 plates are worked out on the following formula: $2^{35} - 1$, i.e. total 34,35,97,38,367 moves. For 10 plates, in one minute 14.61 moves are involved, whereas machine would do 20 times more work in one minute; i.e. it would make 292.28 moves. All this suggests that the task is well nigh impossible.

98. It is our usual experience that every criminal thinks his act will go undetected. But, it is not quite so. The criminal, unknowingly and unwittingly leaves some such clue behind him which ultimately digs his grave. This is a exactly what happened in the case of Badri Nath.

    The gas cylinder gave the first clue. It was exhausted in seven days as against its normal duration of 45 days (Sagar Mal's statement).

    The bulb was on. Prem Das came to the conclusion that Rukmani reached home at 7 and switched on the bulb. Since the knob and the regulator of the cylinder were open the room was filled with gas and the spark, when the bulb was switched on, ignited the pervading gas.

    Other leads: Who opened the knob and the regulator? As per Prem Das's conclusion, it could be none but Badri Nath. As a routine Badri Nath closed his shop at 8 p.m. but reached home at 10 p.m. On the particular day, he came home at 4 p.m. as is established by the statements given by Kamala and the servant of the shop. Badri Nath must have opened the knob and the regulator and left for his shop, reaching there by 4.30 p.m.

99. The details of their earnings are as under :

Fateh Chand	Rs. 5,24,288	Khushi Ram	Rs. 9,83,040
Maturam	Rs. 13,84,448	Seva Nath	Rs. 17,35,680
Dharam Das	Rs. 20,43,008	Roshan Lal	Rs. 23,11,920
Ram Nivas	Rs. 25,47,218	Finally, each had	Rs. 16,47,086

100. None, because the boat rises with the tide.

101. As the liquid would dissolve everything in the world, the problem before Dr. Setu Sadan was, 'Where to keep that liquid."